TATEMS OF CARDIFF

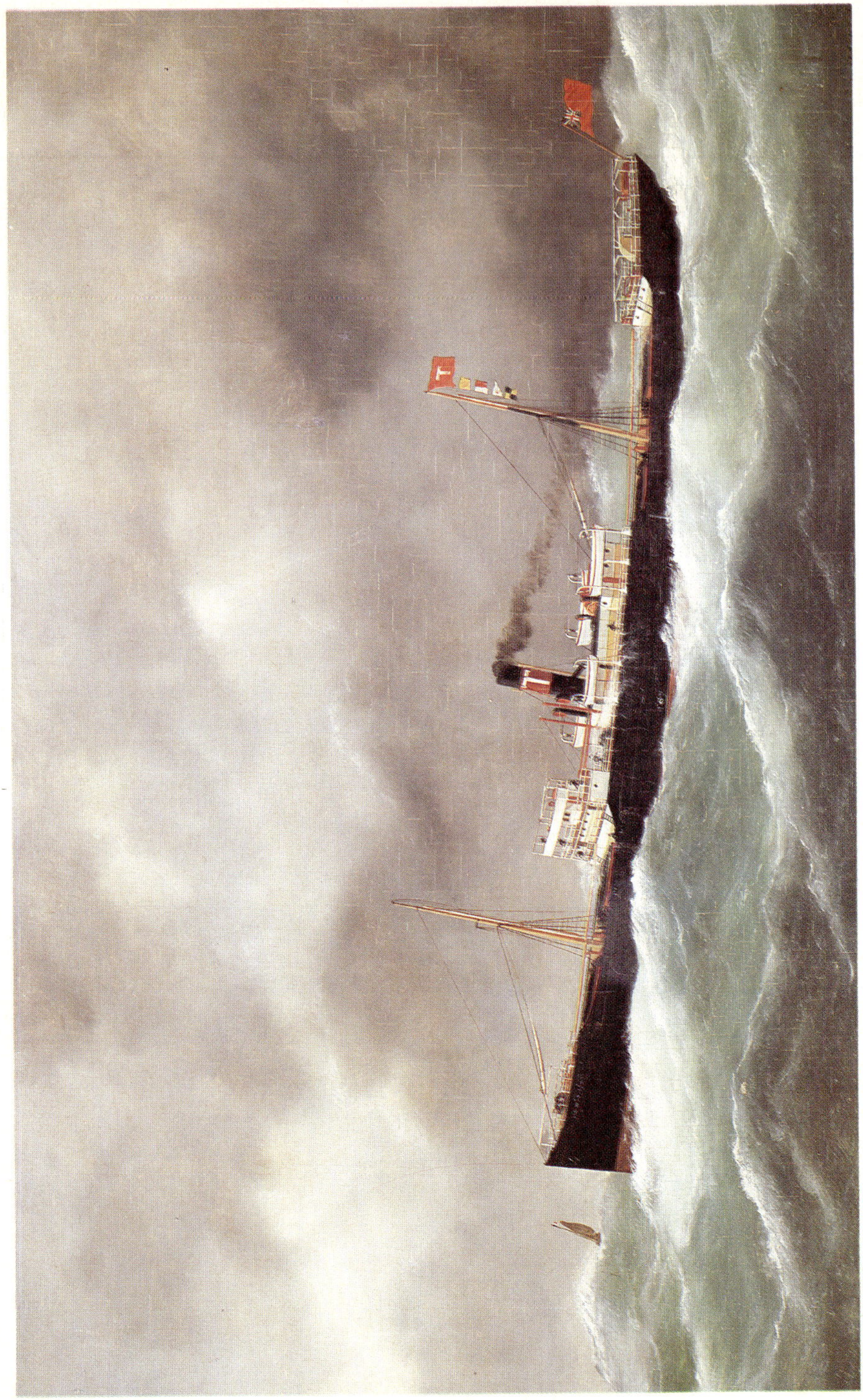

TATEMS OF CARDIFF

by

P. M. HEATON

THE STARLING PRESS LTD.
Printers & Publishers
RISCA   NEWPORT   GWENT
GREAT BRITAIN
1987

ISBN 0 9507714 7 3

© First Edition July, 1987: P. M. Heaton

Published by P. M. Heaton, Pontypool, Gwent, NP4 0QF
Printed by Starling Press Ltd., Risca, Newport, Gwent, NP1 6YB

AUTHOR

Paul Michael Heaton was born at New Inn, Pontypool, in 1944 and was educated at Greenlawn Junior School in New Inn and the Wern Secondary School at Sebastopol. At fifteen he left school and commenced employment, at first in a local store and then with a builders' merchant. A year later he was appointed as a Deck Cadet in the Merchant Navy, with the Lamport and Holt Line of Liverpool, and served in their vessels *Chatham*, *Constable* and *Romney* usually in the Brazil and River Plate trades. He joined the Monmouthshire Constabulary (now Gwent) in 1963 and has served at Abergavenny, Cwmbran, Newport, the Traffic Department and as the Force Public Relations Officer, and now holds the rank of Inspector.

He has always maintained an interest in maritime history, and since 1977 has had numerous articles published in the magazine *Sea Breezes*. He has had the following books published:

Reardon Smith 1905-1980
The Redbrook: A Deep Sea Tramp
The Usk Ships
The Abbey Line
Reardon Smith Line
The South American Saint Line
Welsh Blockade Runners in the Spanish Civil War
Lamport & Holt
The Baron Glanely of St. Fagans and W. J. Tatem Ltd
    (with H. S. Appleyard)
Kaye, Son & Co. Ltd. (with K. O'Donoghue).

ACKNOWLEDGEMENTS

I would like to thank all those who have helped in the compilation of this volume, particularly:—
Major W. D. Gibson, Ross on Wye.
Mr. H. S. Appleyard, Sunderland.
Mr. K. O'Donoghue, Gravesend.
Mr. L. Dunn, Gravesend.
Mr. E. N. Taylor, Gosport.
Mr. Tom Rayner, Ryde, Isle of Wight.
Mr. J. S. Lingwood, Sunderland.
Mr. I. W. Rooke, Heathfield.
Mr. M. Crowdy, Kendal.
Mr. G. H. Somner, Christchurch.
Mr. R. S. Fenton, London.
Mr. R. Hackman.
Mr. C. J. M. Carter, Wirral.
Skyfotos Ltd., New Romney, Kent.
The National Horseracing Museum, Newmarket.
Austin & Pickersgill Ltd., Sunderland.
World Ship Society Central Record Team.
Associated British Ports, Cardiff.
Newport Reference Library.
The National Museum of Wales—Welsh Industrial and Maritime Museum, Cardiff.
A. H. Stockwell Ltd., Ilfracombe, for permission to reproduce material from the book *The Scrap Log of an Engineer* by William Patton.

CONTENTS

Author		5
Acknowledgements		6
List of Illustrations		8
1.	Introduction	11
2.	William James Tatem—His Origins and Early Career	12
3.	The Entry Into Shipowning	13
4.	Further Expansion	19
5.	The First World War	23
6.	Post First World War Developments	25
7.	Lord Glanely's Racing Career	27
8.	The Depression	30
9.	The Spanish Civil War	33
10.	The Late 1930s	37
11.	The Second World War	40
12.	The Post-War Years	42
13.	Appendix One—Fleet List	49
14.	Appendix Two—Ships Owned by the Maritime Shipping and Trading Co. Ltd. (G. C. Gibson)	65
15.	Appendix Three—Ships Managed on behalf of the Ministry of War Transport	66

LIST OF ILLUSTRATIONS

1. Lord Glanely's home—Exning House, Newmarket. *(Welsh Industrial & Maritime Museum).*
2. William James Tatem in 1907. *(Welsh Industrial & Maritime Museum).*
3. Lord Glanely in the 1930s. *(Welsh Industrial & Maritime Museum).*
4. William James Tatem at the laying of the Foundation Stone of St. Stephen's Church, West Bute Street, Cardiff, in 1912. *(Welsh Industrial & Maritime Museum).*
5. Lord Glanely and Sir William Reardon Smith receiving the Freedom of the City of Cardiff, on March 23, 1928. *(Welsh Industrial & Maritime Museum).*
6. Newspaper Boy heralds Lord Glanely's Derby Triumph in 1919. *(Welsh Industrial & Maritime Museum).*
7. Gordon Richards mounted on "Singapore". *(Welsh Industrial & Maritime Museum).*
8. Lord Glanely leading in "Singapore", victorious in the St. Leger, 1930. *(Welsh Industrial & Maritime Museum).*
9. The "Shandon" (1) fitting out at Stockton-on-Tees in 1899. *(Welsh Industrial & Maritime Museum).*
10. The "Wooda" of 1901 undergoing repairs to collison damage in 1915. *(I. W. Rooke).*
11. The "Iddesleigh" was built in 1904 by Richardson, Duck and Company, Stockton-on-Tees. *(Tom Rayner).*
12. The Turret-Deck steamer "Wellington" was a product of William Doxford and Sons Ltd., Sunderland in 1905. *(Welsh Industrial & Maritime Museum).*
13. The "Torrington", with her sistership "Wellington" were the largest ships owned at Cardiff when completed in 1905. *(Welsh Industrial & Maritime Museum).*
14. The "Torrington" with Cardiff's 'Waifs and Strays' on board on the occasion of the opening of the Queen Alexandra Dock in 1907. *(Welsh Industrial & Maritime Museum).*
15. The newly completed "Lady Lewis" (2) with a party of blind children on board at the opening of the Queen Alexandra Dock, Cardiff in 1907. *(I. W. Rooke).*
16. The "Cloutsham" was built for the Tatem Steam Navigation Co. Ltd., in 1910. *(I. W. Rooke).*
17. The "Quantock" of 1910. *(I. W. Rooke).*
18. Craig, Taylor and Co. Ltd., Stockton-on-Tees, completed the "Bideford" in 1910. *(E. N. Taylor)*
19. The "Eggesford" (1) of 1910. *(Tom Rayner).*
20. The "Exford" (1) was captured by the German cruiser "Emden" in October 1914. Retaken a month later by H.M.S "Empress of Asia", she was subsequently renamed "Brendon". She is shown under her later name of "Assunzione". *(Laurence Dunn).*
21. The steamer "Molton" arrived in the fleet in 1919. She was captured by General Franco's Nationalist Navy in the Spanish Civil War whilst attempting to enter Santander in 1937. *(E. N. Taylor).*
22. The "Pilton" of 1920. *(E. N. Taylor).*
23. The steamer "Somerton" of 1920 laid up at Fowey in April, 1933. *(Laurence Dunn).*
24. The "Buckleigh" (2) was built by Bartram and Sons Ltd., Sunderland in 1925. *(E. N. Taylor).*
25. The "Ashleigh" (2) of 1925 laid up at Fowey, September 1933. *(Tom Rayner).*
26. The "Iddesleigh" (2) of 1927 was built for the Tatem Steam Navigation Co. Ltd. *(Tom Rayner).*
27. The "Winkleigh" (1) of 1927. *(E. N. Taylor).*
28. The "Umberleigh" was a product in 1927 of William Gray and Co. Ltd., West Hartlepool. *(Welsh Industrial & Maritime Museum).*
29. The "Monkleigh" of 1927. *(Welsh Industrial & Maritime Museum).*

30. The "Goodleigh" (1) laid up at Fowey in 1933. She was owned by a single-ship company, the Dulverton Steamship Co. Ltd. *(E. N. Taylor)*.
31. The "Filleigh" (1) was built in 1928 by Wm. Pickersgill and Sons Ltd., Sunderland for the Atlantic Shipping and Trading Co. Ltd. *(Tom Rayner)*.
32. The "Appledore" was built in 1929 for G. C. Gibson's Maritime Shipping and Trading Co. Ltd. *(E. N. Taylor)*.
33. The "Everleigh" of 1930. *(Tom Rayner)*.
34. The "Hadleigh" of 1930 laden with timber at Cardiff in 1936. *(Welsh Industrial & Maritime Museum)*.
35. The "Hadleigh". *(E. N. Taylor)*.
36. The "Northleigh" of 1937 seen with a timber cargo before the Second World War. *(Tom Rayner)*.
37. A post-war view of the "Northleigh" at Cardiff. *(Welsh Industrial & Maritime Museum)*.
38. Another view of the "Northleigh". *(Skyfotos Ltd.)*.
39. The "Winkleigh" (2) of 1940 in the English Channel. *(Skyfotos Ltd.)*.
40. The "Winkleigh". *(Welsh Industrial & Maritime Museum)*.
41. The fifth "Chulmleigh" was a product of William Doxford and Sons Ltd., Sunderland. *(Skyfotos Ltd.)*.
42. The Motorship "Chulmleigh" (5). *(Welsh Industrial & Maritime Museum)*.
43. The turbine steamer "Lord Glanely" at Cardiff in 1948. *(Welsh Industrial & Maritime Museum)*.
44. The "Lord Glanely" was delivered by Wm. Pickersgill and Sons Ltd., Sunderland. *(Welsh Industrial & Maritime Museum)*.
45. The "Lord Glanely" in the English Channel. *(Skyfotos Ltd.)*.
46. At 8,261 gross tons, the "Glanely" built by Austin & Pickersgill Ltd., Sunderland, in 1960 was the largest ship to be owned by Tatems. *(Skyfotos Ltd.)*.
47. The "Landwade" of 1961. *(Skyfotos Ltd.)*.
48. Built in 1965 the motorship "Exning" was the last vessel to enter the Tatem fleet. *(Skyfotos Ltd.)*.

1. INTRODUCTION

Looking around Cardiff's Dockland today, it is hard to believe that this was once the greatest coal exporting port in the world. In 1913 coal shipments peaked at a never to be repeated figure of 10½ million tons, and there were over a hundred shipping companies based at the port. One of the biggest fleets locally owned was that of William James Tatem, later to be created Lord Glanely, who operated nineteen ships with a total gross tonnage of 81,467. This was a truly considerable fleet, being all the more amazing when one considers that he had only been a shipowner for sixteen years, and had been born of relatively humble origins.

Apart from his interests in shipping, Lord Glanely later became well known for his involvement in horse racing. He ranked with the select few such as the Aga Khan, Lord Derby, Dorothy Paget and Marcel Boussac who were largely responsible for the high quality racehorses produced between the wars. He was an accomplished owner who won all five Classic races.

With his death in 1942, the business passed to his nephew, George Cock Gibson. In 1973 they withdrew from shipowning, but the business survives today as an investment company in the hands of the third and fourth generations of the family.

In 1980 Harold Appleyard and I wrote a history of the company, entitled *The Baron Glanely of St. Fagans and W. J. Tatem Ltd.* which was published by the World Ship Society. Since then a wealth of additional material has come to light and as a result I decided to compile this expanded volume devoted to the company's history. I am grateful to Harold Appleyard and the Society for permission to use the earlier material.

I have started with an account of the founder's origins and early career, followed by his entry into shipowning, and the various developments over the years. His involvement in horse racing is also covered. I hope that readers will be left with an honest impression of what was involved in the operation of the business over a period of ninety years, and the obvious enterprise of the founder and subsequent generations.

P. M. Heaton.
July, 1987.

2. WILLIAM JAMES TATEM—
HIS ORIGINS AND EARLY CAREER

William James Tatem was born at Appledore, North Devon on March 6, 1868. Sadly whilst still an infant his father died, and as a result his mother Louisa had to set about bringing him and his sister Georgina up on her own. They subsequently moved to Chulmleigh where both received their education.

In view of the family's changed circumstances, when he was old enough he had to set about earning his own living, and not surprisingly in view of Appledore's maritime connections, he chose to go to sea. However, this was not to be successful, in that he suffered a bout of Yellow Fever and was shipwrecked, all in the course of two years. Therefore he looked for another means of supporting himself, and this was in due course to be the making of him.

Disillusioned with the sea he set out for Cardiff where he was successful in gaining employment as a junior clerk in the offices of Messrs. J. H. Anning and Company, the well known tramp shipowners, whose founder also had his origins in Appledore. This firm subsequently became known as Anning Bros. It was here that he gained his early experience in the complexities of ship management which was to be of such great use to him throughout his life.

He married Ada Mary Williams of Pengam Farm, Cardiff on September 14, 1897, just two months after taking delivery of his first ship. They were a devoted couple, but tragically their only child Thomas Shanden Tatem died in 1905 at the early age of six years.

Interestingly his wife's two sisters were also married to men connected with the shipping industry, both of whom were firm friends of Bill Tatem. They were Daniel Radcliffe, whose brother had co-founded the well known tramp shipowners Evan Thomas Radcliffe and Company, and Joseph Frazer who was established as a Ships' Chandler.

3. THE ENTRY INTO SHIPOWNING

Cardiff's position as the world's greatest coal exporting port resulted from heavy investment in the South Wales coalfields and the improved communications brought about by the railways. The result of this development saw a demand worldwide for Welsh steam coal and the construction of the first enclosed dock at Cardiff to facilitate its export. This dock, which became known as the Bute West Dock, was completed in 1839 for the Marquis of Bute, and was followed, as coal shipments increased, by the basin and first section of Bute East Dock in 1855 and the remainder in 1859. This was the first of four major docks completed by 1907, the final being the Queen Alexandra Dock.

From the opening of the first dock in 1839 coal and coke accounted for the greater percentage of total shipments through the port. Some idea of the expansion which took place in trade through the port can be seen in the following table:—

Year	Total Tonnage Handled	Coal & Coke Exports (Tons)	Iron Ore Imports (Tons)
*1839	8,282	6,500	NIL
1840	46,042	43,651	NIL
1850	873,413	661,382	63,085
1860	2,225,980	1,794,005	113,418
1870	2,804,798	2,104,545	119,201
1880	6,291,137	4,843,982	519,976
1886	8,001,588	6,521,956	440,334
1896	10,020,713	7,690,205	682,832

* These figures relate to the New Bute West Dock only.

Young Tatem had commenced his employment in the offices of Anning's in 1886, and was not slow to recognise the remarkable and consistent growth in shipments, particularly of coal and coke. In the following ten years he also saw the growth of shipowning in the port on a large scale. Hitherto the majority of Cardiff's trade had been carried on vessels owned at other ports within the United Kingdom, but as the South Wales coalfields developed, the area attracted newcomers who saw the opportunities to be gained in carrying this expanding trade. This resulted in Cardiff becoming one of the major centres of shipowning in the country.

In consequence of this William James Tatem, early in 1897, decided to enter shipowning on his own account. He formed the firm of W. J. Tatem and Company with offices at 127, Bute Street, Cardiff, and also established the Lady Lewis Steamship Co. Ltd., a public company the shares of which, apart from his own substantial holding, were taken up by friends, relatives and others with an eye to a potentially profitable

The "Lady Lewis" Steamship Company, Limited

STATEMENT OF ACCOUNTS

Dr. Voyage No. 1 from Leaving Builder's yard, July 24th, to October 1st, 1897—69 days. Cr.

	£ s. d.	£ s. d.		£ s. d.	£ s. d.
To Working Expenses:—			By Sundry Freights:—		
Port Charges	1,190 14 6		Cardiff to Venice @ 7/6d	1,549 17 5	
Wages, Provisions & Stores	548 8 10		Nicolaieff and Odessa to Antwerp, average 10/6d per ton	2,404 8 3	
Bunkers	282 17 11				3,954 5 8
		2,022 1 3	,, Mat Money		39 14 6
,, Management & Incidentals		102 11 7	,, Sundry Credits		13 17 1
,, Insurances		415 9 8			
,, Balance, Profit		1,467 14 9			
		£4,007 17 3			£4,007 17 3
			,, Balance, Profit		£1,467 14 9

STATEMENT OF ACCOUNTS
Voyage No. 2

Dr.   October 2nd, 1897, to December 15th, 1897—75 days   **Cr.**

	£ s. d.	£ s. d.		£ s. d.	£ s. d.
To Working Expenses:—			By Sundry Freights:—		
Port Charges............	1,044 10 0		Cardiff to Spezia		
Wages, Provisions & Stores...	507 18 8		Coal @ 6/6d per ton........	1,316 11 6	
Bunkers...............	219 5 0		Sulina to London,		
		1,771 13 8	Mixed Grain @ 10/6d per ton................	2,467 10 0	
,, Management & Incidentals....		100 2 6			3,784 1 6
,, Insurance.............		456 1 3	,, Mat Money............		11 10 0
,, Balance, Profit.............		1,470 9 9	,, Sundry Credits............		2 15 8
		£3,798 7 2			£3,798 7 2
			By Balance, Profit............		£1,470 9 9

The above Balance Sheet for Voyages 1 and 2, covering a period of 144 days, commencing from the time the Steamer left the Builder's Yard, show a profit of £2,938 4s. 6d., out of which I have paid the Shareholders £10 per each £100 share, being at the rate of 25½ per cent per annum.

W. J. TATEM

I have examined the foregoing Accounts and Vouchers for the Voyages, and certify same to be correct.

Cardiff, December 24th, 1897

J. M. LEWIS, F.P.A. Auditor.

investment. Of these latter shareholders the new company attracted many from the North Devon area and Appledore and Bideford in particular. At the same time an order was placed with Richardson, Duck and Company, of Stockton-on-Tees for the construction of a steamship of 5,500 tons deadweight. The ship was launched on June 17, 1897 and duly completed a month later and was named *Lady Lewis* (2,950 gross tons). She was commanded on her maiden voyage and subsequent seven voyages by another Appledore man, Captain William Reardon Smith, who had previously served with Anning Bros. and was later to enter shipowning himself.

The *Lady Lewis* sailed from the builder's yard on July 24, 1897 in ballast to Cardiff where she loaded a cargo of coal for Venice, thereafter she sailed in ballast for the Black Sea where she loaded a cargo of grain at Nicolaieff and Odessa destined for Antwerp. Thereafter she sailed for Cardiff in ballast, arriving on October 1. This first voyage had been undertaken at a favourable freight rate and the founder was well pleased with the result. The ship quickly loaded a cargo of coal which was consigned to Spezia, and then passed into the Black Sea where a full cargo of mixed grain was loaded at Sulina for London. Following discharge the ship sailed for Cardiff in ballast where she arrived on December 14, 1897.

Such was the profitability of these first two voyages by the *Lady Lewis* that the founder declared a dividend of £10 for every £100 share held, which for a 144 day period of trading worked out at 25½% per annum. A result which pleased shareholders, and of which William James Tatem could be justly proud. The full accounts for these first two voyages are reproduced in full.

The Lady Lewis Steamship Co. Ltd. was the first of sixteen single ship companies formed by William James Tatem during the next eight years, and all were managed by him trading as W. J. Tatem and Company, and assisted initially only by a single secretary, a Mr. Williams.

At this time he was involved primarily with the trade from South Wales to Italy with coal and returning to Europe with grain from the Black Sea, but as the fleet was built up, and the individual size of vessels increased, an ever greater involvement with the River Plate trade was undertaken, the ships taking 'coal out/grain home', the stable trade of the South Wales tramp for a number of decades.

Such was the success of the *Lady Lewis*, that an order was placed with Richardson, Duck and Company, Stockton-on-Tees for a second ship, which was duly completed in September, 1898 as the *Sir W. T. Lewis* (3,517 gross tons). These first two steamers were named after the manager of Cardiff's Bute Docks, Sir William Thomas Lewis, and his wife, although the majority of vessels that were to follow were given names of towns and villages in Devon.

The majority of the ships which were built to the order of the companies under the control of W. J. Tatem over the years were built on the North East Coast and included seventeen from the yard of Richardson, Duck and Company, Stockton-on-Tees, who it is interesting to note built the first fourteen vessels, as follows:—

Name	Year Built	Gross Tons	Owning Company
Lady Lewis	1897	2,950	Lady Lewis Steamship Co. Ltd.
Sir W. T. Lewis	1898	3,517	Sir W. T. Lewis Steamship Co. Ltd.
Shandon (1)	1899	3,850	Shandon Steamship Co. Ltd.
Chulmleigh (1)	1900	3,997	Chulmleigh Steamship Co. Ltd.
Southport	1900	3,588	Southport Steamship Co. Ltd.
Westward Ho	1900	3,596	Westward Ho Steamship Co. Ltd.
Wooda	1901	3,804	Wooda Steamship Co. Ltd.
Chorley	1901	3,828	Chorley Steamship Co. Ltd.
Appledore (1)	1901	3,843	Appledore Steamship Co. Ltd.
Torridge (1)	1902	3,838	Torridge Steamship Co. Ltd.
Northam	1902	3,842	Northam Steamship Co. Ltd.
Dunster	1902	4,662	Dunster Steamship Co. Ltd.
Dulverton	1904	4,508	Dulverton Steamship Co. Ltd.
Iddesleigh (1)	1904	4,027	Iddesleigh Steamship Co. Ltd.

As can be seen Tatem's third ship was the steamer *Shandon* which was completed in June, 1899. Captain William Reardon Smith transferred from the steamer *Lady Lewis* to take over command of the new vessel for her maiden and two subsequent voyages. He left the vessel at Manchester on April 4, 1900, and indeed left the sea for good to take up various business interests at Cardiff prior to entering shipowning himself in 1905.

Tatem was a clever individual who was able to see opportunities and seize them for his own advantage and that of his shareholders. He generated great confidence and it was in this manner that he was able to create such a large fleet of ships, which in 1904 stood at fourteen vessels.

The total tonnage handled at Cardiff in 1897, the year Tatem had entered shipowning, was at its highest level up to that date; a year later, however, it dropped significantly, but recovered in 1899 and remained more or less constant for the next six years, as the following table shows:—

Year	Total Tonnage Handled	Coal & Coke Exports (Tons)	Iron Ore Imports (Tons)
1897	10,238,785	7,722,995	734,131
1898	7,498,574	5,652,666	484,058
1899	10,975,731	8,279,005	825,548
1904	10,271,018	7,490,481	806,164

In 1902 the firm's offices were moved from 127, Bute Street, Cardiff to Phoenix Buildings, Mount Stuart Square and in 1909 to Cambrian Buildings, Mount Stuart Square, and in 1927 to much larger premises at the National Provincial Bank Building, 113-116, Bute Street, Cardiff.

4. FURTHER EXPANSION

Tatem had built up a fine fleet of modern steamships in the eight years prior to 1905. All fourteen vessels had come from the Stockton-on-Tees yard of Richardson, Duck and Company, but in 1905 he decided to order two turret deck steamers from William Doxford and Sons Ltd., Sunderland, which were duly delivered later the same year as the *Wellington* and *Torrington* and were registered in the ownership of single ship companies which took their titles from the names of the vessels. At 5,600 gross tons they were the largest vessels to enter the fleet and were indeed the biggest ships registered at Cardiff. It is also interesting to note that at this time Tatem was operating the largest fleet owned at the port. This was a considerable achievement when it is realised that he had only been engaged in shipowning for eight years, and says much for his ability as a businessman.

The first loss suffered by the firm occurred on April 3, 1906, when the pioneer vessel *Lady Lewis* was wrecked near Mogotes Point whilst on passage from Bahia Blanca to Barcelona with a cargo of grain. The three year old *Dulverton* represented the second loss when she left Bahia Blanca for Antwerp with a cargo of grain on April 13, 1907. She was sighted by the Cardiff steamer *Lesreaulx* four days later when she was stopped with engine trouble, but her master declined an offer of assistance, and nothing more was ever heard of the ship or her crew.

During 1907 Richardson, Duck and Company completed a replacement for the first *Lady Lewis* which was given the same name. This ship was a fine vessel of 3,477 gross tons, and had the distinction of being the first vessel to enter the new Queen Alexandra Dock at Cardiff in 1907 when it was officially opened by King George V. On this occasion a party of blind children were carried as a treat. The steamer *Torrington* followed carrying a large number of Cardiff's "Waifs and Strays", this being a charity with which Bill Tatem had become heavily involved following the sad loss of his only son.

On December 29, 1909 the steamer *Shandon* stranded 1½ miles South East of Heligoland whilst on passage from Odessa to the River Weser. She was refloated early the following year, but it was decided to dispose of the ship which was sold to German owners, thereafter she had a long career finally being broken up in 1930. The next loss suffered by the firm was the *Torridge* which on April 18, 1910 was wrecked on Farquhar Island whilst on passage from Port Natal to Galle, Ceylon in ballast.

Early in 1910 it was decided to amalgamate the fifteen single ship companies which at that time actually owned a vessel, into one company, the Tatem Steam Navigation Co. Ltd. which had a capital of £350,000.

The Dulverton Steamship Co. Ltd. which had been without a vessel since the loss of its steamer in 1907 was retained for the future.

Five ships arrived in the fleet during 1910; the *Cloutsham* (4,907 gross tons) and *Quantock* (4,470 gross tons) from William Doxford and Sons Ltd., Sunderland, the *Bideford* and *Eggesford* both of 3,560 gross tons from Craig, Taylor and Co. Ltd., Stockton-on-Tees, and the *Bampton* of 4,496 gross tons from Richardson, Duck and Company. A year later the *Exford* and *Braunton* each of 4,500 gross tons were completed by Craig, Taylor and Co. Ltd. and Richardson, Duck and Company, respectively. The final ship to join the fleet prior to the First World War was the *Torridge* (2) (5,036 gross tons) from the yard of Bartram and Sons Ltd., Sunderland.

In 1911, after a mere four years in the fleet the steamer *Lady Lewis* (2) was disposed of, passing to Australian owners as the *Yankalilla*, in 1929 she went to the Swedish flag at the *Bolivia* and was later renamed *Pluto*, finally hoisting the Finish flag in 1933. She was torpedoed and sunk by the German submarine *U146* on June 28, 1941 100 miles NNW of the Butt of Lewis.

Prior to the First World War, four other ships were disposed of to other owners. In 1912 the steamer *Southport* was sold to the Lewis Trading Co. Ltd., a company managed by T. Lewis of Cardiff. On September 4, 1914 the ship was captured by the German cruiser *Geier* off the Caroline Islands. The crew of the raider immobilised the ship's engine whilst she pursued other shipping, but the crew succeeded in repairing her and arrived at Brisbane on September 30. She survived thereafter until broken up in 1932.

The *Westward Ho* passed to the Lewis Maritime Co. Ltd., Cardiff in 1913, this being another company managed by T. Lewis. In 1916 she was sold to other British owners for whom she traded as the *Baywest*, but became a victim of a tragic accident when on September 9, 1918 she was struck by a shell from a French steamer 1½ miles W. by S. from the Longships, Cornwall, whilst on a voyage from Fort de France to Marseilles. As a result she caught fire and was sunk as a derelict.

The *Sir W. T. Lewis* passed to Greek owners in 1913 and survived until on November 29, 1940 she reported that she was in distress in position 46.53′N, 48.37′W whilst on passage to Belfast, and was presumed to have foundered in a gale, with the tragic loss of all hands. The *Eggesford* which was sold in 1914 also passed to the Greek flag, and survived until on December 1, 1942 she sank off New York following a collision with the Panamanian steamer *Intrepido*.

The year 1913 was the most prosperous in Cardiff's history in that coal shipments peaked at 10½ million tons out of 13 million tons of total tonnage handled. This was a figure which was never to be repeated. The following figures show the increase in trade since 1905.

Year	Total Tonnage Handled	Coal & Coke Exports (Tons)	Iron Ore Imports (Tons)
1905	10,189,831	7,294,020	876,457
1913	13,054,419	10,576,506	746,381

Iron ore shipments had decreased slightly, but this was more because other South Wales ports, particularly Newport, tended to handle this commodity. Cardiff was, however, handling increasing quantities of prepared timber and pitwood.

Up to this point the management of the fleet was still undertaken by William James Tatem himself, but on July 14, 1913 he formed the firm of W. J. Tatem Ltd. to act as managers. This private company had a paid up capital of 100,000 £1 shares of which the founder held 97,999 shares.

5. THE FIRST WORLD WAR

At the outbreak of the First World War the fleet totalled sixteen vessels and during the period of hostilities a further six were added. Of these, nine ships were lost as a result of enemy action and five were disposed of to other owners.

On October 19, 1914 the German cruiser *Emden* captured the *Exford* (1) in the Indian Ocean and placed a prize crew on board her. On learning of the loss of the vessel the company allocated the name to a new building which had been purchased on the stocks at Bartram and Sons Ltd., Sunderland. However, on December 11 the same year, H.M.S. *Empress of Asia* recaptured the original *Exford* and took her to Singapore where early the following year she was handed back to the company. Thus for a short period there were two ships of the same name in the fleet but this was resolved by renaming the earlier vessel *Brendon*.

Apart from the *Exford* (2) which was acquired during 1914, another ship was bought. This was a 4,414 gross ton steamer which was in course of construction at R. Thompson and Sons Ltd., Sunderland, as the *Recina* for Austrian owners. At the outbreak of hostilities the ship had been seized on the stocks as a war prize, and it was in these circumstances that Tatem acquired her. She was completed as the *Eggesford* (2).

The first loss suffered by the company as a result of enemy action was the *Honiton* which had only been delivered in May, 1915 by A. McMillan and Son Ltd., Dumbarton. Whilst homeward bound from Buenos Aires to Hull on her maiden voyage she was mined off the Longsand Light Vessel on August 30, 1915 and in a damaged condition was beached at Shoeburyness where she was subsequently declared a constructive total loss.

As a result of the war, the demand for tonnage worldwide had increased considerably. Individual owners were allowed to continue fixing cargoes for their ships for the first three years of the war and this resulted in considerable profits being made, as freight rates rocketed. This meant that ships were changing hands at double or treble their pre-war values. In these circumstances Tatem decided to dispose of four of his ships in order to take advantage of the rise in values.

The *Chulmleigh*, *Wooda* and *Dunster* were sold to Brys and Gylsen Ltd., the London based section of a Belgian owner, whilst the *Northam* passed to Harris and Dixon Ltd. of London, who a year later resold her to the owner of the other three vessels. The *Dunster* was only to have a short career as on February 15, 1916 she was abandoned on fire in position 39.01′N, 67.00′W, following an explosion amongst cylinders of chlorine gas in her cargo whilst on a voyage from New York to Havre. The *Northam* was to have a succession of owners before she was broken up in

Italy in 1931. The *Chulmleigh* and *Wooda* were both lost through marine hazard in 1931. The former vessel was wrecked on Pearl Rock on January 26 whilst on a voyage from Fellonica to Amsterdam with a cargo of pyrites, whilst the latter sank on June 30 20 miles North of Cape Ivi, Algeria, after stranding near Tenes whilst on a voyage from La Goulette to Dunkirk with iron ore.

During 1916 the steamer *Chorley* was also sold to Brys and Gylsen Ltd., but she was lost the following year when on March 22 she was torpedoed and sunk by the German submarine *UC48* 25 miles E. by S. of Start Point.

On April 7, 1916 the *Braunton* was torpedoed and sunk by the submarine *UB29* off Beachy Head whilst on a voyage from Boulogne to Newport with Government stores. The same submarine was also responsible for the next loss when on September 6, 1916 the *Torridge* (2) was captured 40 miles from Start Point and sunk by bombs whilst on a voyage from Genoa to the River Tyne in ballast. The steamer *Eggesford* (2) was more fortunate, as on November 30 of the same year she was captured by a submarine 30 miles North from Ushant, the crew of which placed bombs on board which badly damaged the ship. However, the ship did not sink, and the *Eggesford's* crew who had taken to the boats reboarded the vessel after the submarine had left the scene, and eventually with the assistance of tugs she was towed into port. Following repairs she was returned to service in the Tatem fleet.

During 1916 A. McMillan and Son Ltd., Dumbarton delivered a 4,911 gross ton steamer, the *Chulmleigh* (2) to the Tatem fleet followed a year later by a sister ship the *Buckleigh*. In 1917 the largest ship to enter the fleet up to that point arrived from the Stockton-on-Tees yard of Ropner and Sons Ltd. The ship was named *Ashleigh* and was of 6,985 gross tons.

Meanwhile, on December 7, 1916 a new company, the Atlantic Shipping and Trading Co. Ltd. was formed and early in 1917 the entire fleet was transferred to the new company, thus leaving the Tatem Steam Navigation Co. Ltd. temporarily without any ships. At about this time an office was opened in London and the registry of the ships transferred from Cardiff to London.

On January 7, 1917 the steamer *Bampton* had a lucky escape when she was chased by a submarine off the coast of Portugal. She was fortunate at being able to outrun the enemy vessel by using her greater speed.

The most tragic loss of the war was the turret-deck steamer *Torrington* which was torpedoed and sunk by the German submarine *U55* 150 miles South West of the Scilly Isles. Her crew put to the boats, and nothing was ever heard of the Chief Officer's boat. However the Master was directed by the submarine to pull alongside where he was taken prisoner. Meanwhile the crew of the *Torrington* boarded the submarine's deck, where they remained and were drowned when the enemy vessel submerged.

Only the master of the Tatem ship survived, and the details of the loss were not revealed until he was repatriated from Germany after the end of hostilities. Tragically her complement of thirty-four men were all lost.

Later the same month, on April 25 the steamer *Bideford* was to be more fortunate, when she was slightly damaged by gunfire from a German torpedo boat off Dunkirk. The following day the *Quantock* was torpedoed by a submarine off Fastnet, but fortunately the ship remained afloat and was towed in where she was repaired and subsequently returned to service. Sadly two lives were lost.

Two months later on June 9, the steamer *Appledore* was to be less fortunate, as she was torpedoed and sunk by the submarine *U70* when 164 miles South by West from the Fastnet. On July 14 the *Exford* (2) was torpedoed and sunk 180 miles from Ushant by *U48*, with the tragic loss of six members of her crew. The newly completed *Ashleigh* was torpedoed and sunk 290 miles South West from the Fastnet by *U54* on July 23, and on September 14 the *Chulmleigh* (2), after less than one year in the fleet, was torpedoed and sunk by *U64* off Cape Salou, Spain.

On October 19, 1917 the turret-deck steamer *Wellington* was torpedoed in the English Channel, and although damaged managed to make port. Similarly the *Eggesford* (2) was torpedoed in the Mediterranean on January 31, 1918 but managed to reach port where repairs were effected.

The final war loss was the *Wellington* which on September 16, 1918 was torpedoed and sunk off Cape Villano by *U118* with the tragic loss of five lives including her Master.

On July 13, 1916 in recognition of his contribution to the war effort, in raising war loans and recruitment etc., William James Tatem had been created a Baronet and on June 28, 1918 he was elevated to the Peerage, taking the title of The Baron Glanely of St. Fagans.

6. POST FIRST WORLD WAR DEVELOPMENTS

At the conclusion of hostilities the Atlantic Shipping and Trading Co. Ltd. had a fleet of eight ships as follows:—

Name	Year Built	Gross Tons
Iddesleigh (1)	1904	4,027
Cloutsham	1910	4,907
Quantock	1910	4,470
Bideford	1910	3,562
Bampton	1910	4,496
Brendon (ex *Exford* (1))	1911	4,542
Eggesford (2)	1914	4,414
Buckleigh (1)	1917	4,920

The arrival of peace heralded a short period of great prosperity for the shipping industry as markets neglected in the war were restocked by industry returning to peace time production and as a result freight rates rocketed. In consequence the price being paid for ships was very high and in view of this Lord Glanely decided to take advantage of the situation and in 1919 disposed of the entire fleet of eight ships which had survived the war which resulted in handsome dividends to shareholders.

Seven of the ships passed to Mediterranean Cargo Steamers Ltd. of London, who under the management of W. J. Foster operated a service between the United Kingdom and Southern Spain and Italy. The steamer *Bideford* passed to H. Roberts and Son's North Wales Shipping Co. Ltd. and was eventually renamed *North Anglia* and registered at Newcastle. She was torpedoed and sunk whilst under the Greek flag in 1942.

However, during 1919 and 1920 six new ships were acquired of which two were from the Ropner Shipbuilding and Repairing Co. (Stockton) Ltd. and four from the British Government, as follows:—

Name	Year Built	Gross Tons
Shandon (2)	1919	3,069
Molton	1919	3,091
Monkton	1920	3,088
Pilton	1920	3,063
Paignton/Notton	1920	3,096
Somerton	1920	5,227

Three of the ships were acquired by Lord Glanely on his own account and one each by the Tatem Steam Navigation Co. Ltd., the Atlantic Shipping and Trading Co. Ltd. and W. J. Tatem Ltd. By the middle of

1920 five of these ships were registered in the ownership of the Atlantic Shipping and Trading Co. Ltd. and one with a new company, the Foreland Shipping and Trading Co. Ltd., but the following year this latter company's ship had passed to the ownership of the Atlantic Shipping and Trading Co. Ltd.

The prosperous period following the First World War was declining somewhat by 1921 and the founder's decision to keep the fleet at less than half the pre-war size was vindicated. By 1922 there were many South Wales shipowners who were in serious financial difficulties but by careful management the position of the companies under the control of Lord Glanely had remained secure. However, in order not to put the capital of his friends and associates in the Atlantic Shipping and Trading Co. Ltd. at risk, he transferred the ownership of all six ships to W. J. Tatem Ltd. The Atlantic Shipping and Trading Co. Ltd. was a public company with numerous shareholders whereas W. J. Tatem Ltd. was a private, limited company of which the founder virtually held all the shares. Thus, during these difficult years, Lord Glanely took the entire risk on his own account.

It should be pointed out that the fleet disposed of in 1919 was of the type and size of vessel most suitable for the River Plate trade, whereas five of the six ships acquired, being of a smaller size, were more suitable for the Mediterranean and Intermediate tramp trades.

In 1912 Mr. George Cock Gibson, Lord Glanely's nephew, had joined the firm at Cardiff, but had left to serve in the war. However at the end of hostilities he had returned and in 1919 formed his own company, the Maritime Shipping and Trading Co. Ltd. He acquired a 5,264 gross ton war built steamer from the British Government for £220,000 which he, together with Messrs. H. G. Cox and A. E. Rice, renamed *Cutcombe*, and managed thereafter under his own name.

7. LORD GLANELY'S RACING CAREER

Lord Glanely was a worthy citizen and was a Justice of the Peace, a Doctor of Law (University of South Wales and Monmouthshire), Deputy Lieutenant of Glamorgan, High Sheriff of Glamorgan for 1911/12 and received the Freedom of the City of Cardiff in 1928. His various offices included Chairman of Cardiff Race Club, President of Cardiff Shipowners Association for 1907, President of the Royal Hamadryad Seamen's Hospital, the Royal Porthcawl Golf Club and the University of South Wales and Monmouthshire for the years 1920 to 1925 and 1934 to 1942. He was a Director of the Great Western Railway, Mount Stuart Dry Docks Ltd., Ropner Shipbuilding and Repairing Co. (Stockton) Ltd., Lobitos Oilfields Ltd., Anglo-Ecuadorian Oilfields Ltd., British Corporation Register of Shipping and Aircraft, West of England Protection and Indemnity Association, The Shipping Federation, Cardiff Exchange Ltd., The Coal and Shipping Exchange (Cardiff) Ltd., British Steamship Owners Association and the Chepstow Racecourse Company, of which he was a founder.

He had a passion for racehorses and was a distinguished owner who won all five Classic races. He became a member of the Jockey Club and eventually took up residence at Exning House, Exning, Newmarket.

His career as an owner of thoroughbreds, and his record as a breeder, had a profound influence upon the British Turf during the inter-war years. Initially his interest was in Hackneys and Hunters, but in 1908 he transferred his major interest to the thoroughbred. He entered the ranks of owners when he purchased at Newmarket October Sales the yearling colt *Green Wood*, the first racehorse to run in his name. Other animals owned by Lord Glanely in 1909 were *Glen Clova, Goemon, Royal Stone* and *St. Vitus*. However, only *Goemon* was successful; he was his first winner, when, as a four year old, he won the Ford Manor Handicap at Lingfield Park in June, 1909.

In 1911 he won his first notable race with the *Rock Egg* colt, afterwards named *Quantock* which was successful in the Sefton Park Plate at Liverpool, and in the same year won at Birmingham and Derby. From that time he became an increasingly prominent supporter of the Turf. His first racing jacket was "dark blue, white yoke, sleeves and cap". In 1911 he registered new colours—"black, red, white, and blue belt and cap", which became well known, and to this day are carried by his great nephew's stable—Major William David Gibson.

Following the First World War he appointed Francis Barling as his private trainer at Falmouth House, Newmarket. In 1919 the stable was most successful when *Grand Parade* won the Derby and seven of his horses won at Royal Ascot. During this time he entered the bloodstock world in a big way, and in the same year he set a new record price for a yearling paying 11,500 guineas for *Westward Ho*. The following year, 1920, he topped this giving 14,500 guineas for *Blue Ensign*, although the latter never won a race.

He had acquired Danebury House, Newmarket in 1918 as a Stud Farm, and in 1920 purchased Lagrange Stables at Newmarket, installing a number of private trainers in succession, before ending up with Captain Thomas Hogg in 1928. Two years later he won the Oaks with *Rose of England* and the St. Leger with *Singapore*. These two were eventually mated resulting in *Chulmleigh* which won the 1937 St. Leger.

In 1934 he won the 2,000 guineas with *Columbo*, ridden by W. R. Johnstone, who had been given a retainer at the end of the previous season. This arrangement only lasted a season following the poor ride which Johnstone gave the colt in the Derby (he finished third). In 1938 Basil Jarvis took over Lord Glanely's horses following the retirement of Captain Hogg due to ill health. This partnership continued until the outbreak of the Second World War when, because Lagrange was requisitioned by the Army, Lord Glanely moved his horses to J. Lawson's yard at Manton. It was from here that he gained his final classic win with *Dancing Time* in the substitute 1,000 guineas.

The following table gives some idea of Lord Glanely's exceptional record as an owner:—

ANNUAL RECORD AS OWNER

1909-1937

Total Stakes Won...£264,171.6s.10d.
Races 485

Year	Stakes Won £. s. d.	Races
1909	100 0 0	1
1910	325 0 0	3
1911	1,921 0 0	6
1912	664 0 0	6
1913	2,233 0 0	11
1914	387 0 0	3
1915	527 0 0	3
1916	3,608 0 0	8
1917	2,941 0 0	9

Year	Stakes Won £. s. d.	Races
1918	6,626 12 6	16
1919	30,604 10 0	45
1920	5,509 0 0	15
1921	3,726 0 0	8
1922	3,942 0 0	9
1923	6,014 0 0	13
1924	5,814 0 0	10
1925	11,482 0 0	24
1926	9,565 0 0	25
1927	10,613 0 0	29
1928	14,387 0 0	34
1929	9,393 0 0	25
1930	40,491 0 0	38
1931	12,547 5 0	27
1932	8,043 3 4	19
1933	24,552 15 0	28
1934	16,160 10 0	21
1935	7,601 0 0	13
1936	7,374 10 0	14
1937	17,019 1 0	22
GRAND TOTALS	264,171 6 10	485

THE GREAT YEARS

1919 — First in List of Winning Owners	(£30,604)
1930 — Second in List of Winning Owners	(£40,491)
1933 — Second in List of Winning Owners	(£24,552)
1934 — Second in List of Winning Owners	(£16,160)

I do not have details for the period 1938/42.

8. THE DEPRESSION

Although Lord Glanely had built up a large fleet prior to the First World War, he was an alert man who was quick to assess the right moment to reduce his fleet. He foresaw the crash of the early 1920s, and had sold his entire fleet at the height of the boom when the greatest possible return was achieved. He had, in contrast to most other owners, realised at a very early stage that success in such a cyclical industry as shipping was to be achieved by not having all one's investments actually in ships. As a result he had built up substantial reserves, had a moderately sized modern fleet in the early twenties and had considerable investments outside the shipping industry, including 3,500 acres of land at Newmarket. From the end of the First World War his investments and reserves were always to be far in excess of the asset value of his ships, and it was little wonder that he was always able to pay a dividend to shareholders even in the most difficult years. This was a record which very few others were able to achieve.

In 1923 he decided to take advantage of a good offer which was made for the steamer *Notton* (ex *Paignton*), and as a result the ship passed to French owners. This left five ships in the fleet, all of which were registered in the ownership of the management company—W. J. Tatem Ltd.

Having weathered the worst of the difficult years in the early 1920s and not having added any new tonnage for five years, it was decided to order a number of ships suitable for worldwide tramping which were all built on the North East Coast and were given names taken from Devon with the 'leigh' suffix. The Tatem Steam Navigation Co. Ltd. which had not owned a ship for five years took delivery of the three ships built in 1925 and the four built in 1927. The Atlantic Shipping and Trading Co. Ltd. which had not owned tonnage for six years took delivery of one ship built in 1928 and two vessels completed in 1930, whilst a single ship completed in 1928 was delivered to the Dulverton Steamship Co. Ltd. Thus by 1930, even accounting for the sale of the *Monkton* the previous year, the fleet managed by W. J. Tatem Ltd. totalled fifteen ships, all of which had been built since the First World War, as follows:—

Name	Year Built	Gross Tons
Shandon (2)	1919	3,069
Molton	1919	3,091
Pilton	1920	3,063
Somerton	1920	5,227
Buckleigh (2)	1925	5,074
Chulmleigh (3)	1925	5,076

Name	Year Built	Gross Tons
Ashleigh (2)	1925	4,853
Iddesleigh (2)	1927	5,205
Winkleigh (1)	1927	5,055
Umberleigh	1927	4,950
Monkleigh	1927	5,203
Goodleigh (1)	1928	3,845
Filleigh (1)	1928	4,856
Everleigh	1930	5,222
Hadleigh	1930	5,222

Good connections had been built up at Vancouver, and an ever greater involvement with the lumber trade from this region took place. In addition to general tramping, the River Plate, Baltic and Mediterranean trades were also served.

During 1928 George Gibson disposed of the Maritime Shipping and Trading Company's vessel *Cutcombe* and in 1929 replaced her with the *Appledore* (2), a new building from the Furness Shipbuilding Co. Ltd., which he appropriately registered at the North Devon port of Bideford. Mr. Gibson was the Company Secretary of W. J. Tatem Ltd. from September 6, 1929 until April 20, 1931, and was appointed a director on July 12, 1930.

Such were the difficulties created by the depression of the early 1930s that Lord Glanely decided to sell two of the ships built in 1925. Thus in 1933 the *Buckleigh* (2) and *Chulmleigh* (3) passed to the Scindia Steam Navigation Co. Ltd., of Bombay, as the *Jalamohan* and *Jalarajan* respectively. The former was subsequently broken up in 1951 at Bombay, whilst the latter vessel was torpedoed and sunk on January 14, 1942 by the Japanese submarine *I165* whilst on passage from Singapore to Calcutta.

With the sale of these two ships at what was regarded as a quite respectable price, the fleet stood at thirteen. The lack of cargo for shipment, and the apparent contraction of the coal trade from South Wales coupled with extremely poor freight rates resulted in long periods of lay up for the fleet. In September, 1933 only the three year old steamer *Hadleigh* was still trading, the remainder being laid up as follows:—

FOWEY

Ashleigh, Filleigh, Goodleigh, Iddesleigh, Umberleigh and *Somerton*.

CARDIFF

Everleigh, Monkleigh and *Molton*.

BARRY

Winkleigh and *Shandon*.

MILFORD HAVEN
Pilton.

In 1934 the steamer *Shandon* was sold to Turkish owners for whom she traded for many years. She was followed in 1935 by the *Somerton* which passed to the Greek flag. In 1954 she was sold to owners domiciled in Costa Rica. On November 3, 1958 she arrived at Rotterdam with a cargo of timber from Yxpila, having developed leaks and grounded during the voyage. After discharging her cargo she was laid up at the port, and early the following year was broken up at Hendrik Ido Ambacht.

Gradually the freight market recovered sufficiently to bring the fleet out of lay up, but in 1936 Lord Glanely took advantage of a good offer for the eleven year old *Ashleigh* (2) from Counties Ship Management Co. Ltd. of London, thereafter she had a succession of owners, surviving until 1962 when she was broken up at Osaka. In 1937 the smaller *Goodleigh* (1) was sold to German owners. This ship was seized at Botwood on September 10, 1939 as a war prize, and was subsequently placed under the Ministry of War Transport as the *Empire Commerce*. On June 9, 1940 she was mined and sunk 4 cables from Spit Buoy, near Margate.

This temporarily reduced the Tatem fleet to nine ships.

Lord Glanely's home—Exning House, Newmarket.

(Welsh Industrial & Maritime Museum)

William James Tatem in 1907.   (Welsh Industrial & Maritime Museum)

Lord Glanely in the 1930s. (Welsh Industrial & Maritime Museum)

William James Tatem at the laying of the Foundation Stone of St. Stephen's Church, West Bute Street, Cardiff, in 1912. (Welsh Industrial & Maritime Museum)

Lord Glanely and Sir William Reardon Smith receiving the Freedom of the City of Cardiff, on March 23, 1928.
(Welsh Industrial & Maritime Museum)

Newspaper Boy heralds Lord Glanely's Derby Triumph in 1919.
Welsh Industrial & Maritime Museum)

Gordon Richards mounted on "Singapore". (Welsh Industrial & Maritime Museum)

Lord Glanely Leading in "Singapore", victorious in the St. Leger, 1930.
(Welsh Industrial & Maritime Museum)

The "Shandon" (1) fitting out at Stockton-on-Tees in 1899. (Welsh Industrial & Maritime Museum)

The "Wooda" of 1901 undergoing repairs to collison damage in 1915.

(I. W. Rooke)

The "Iddesleigh" was built in 1904 by Richardson, Duck and Company, Stockton-on-Tees. (Tom Rayner)

The Turret-Deck steamer "Wellington" was a product of William Doxford & Sons Ltd., Sunderland in 1905.
(Welsh Industrial & Maritime Museum)

The "Torrington" with her sistership "Wellington" were the largest ships owned at Cardiff when completed in 1905.
(Welsh Industrial & Maritime Museum)

The "Torrington" with Cardiff's 'Waifs and Strays' on board on the occasion of the opening of the Queen Alexandra Dock in 1907.

(Welsh Industrial & Maritime Museum)

The newly completed "Lady Lewis" (2) with a party of blind children on board at the opening of the Queen Alexandra Dock, Cardiff in 1907.

(I. W. Rooke)

The "Cloutsham" was built for the Tatem Steam Navigation Co. Ltd., in 1910.

(I. W. Rooke)

The "Quantock" of 1910. (I. W. Rooke)

Craig, Taylor and Co. Ltd., Stockton-on-Tees, completed the "Bideford" in 1910. (E. N. Taylor)

The "Eggesford" (1) of 1910. (Tom Rayner)

The "Exford" (1) was captured by the German cruiser "Emden" in October 1914. Retaken a month later by H.M.S. "Empress of Asia", she was subsequently renamed "Brendon". She is shown under her later name of "Assunzione".
(Laurence Dunn)

The steamer "Molton" arrived in the fleet in 1919. She was captured by General Franco's Nationalist Navy in the Spanish Civil War whilst attempting to enter Santander in 1937.

(E. N. Taylor)

The "Pilton" of 1920. (E. N. Taylor)

The steamer "Somerton" of 1920 laid up at Fowey in April, 1933.

(Laurence Dunn)

The "Buckleigh" (2) was built by Bartram and Sons Ltd., Sunderland in 1925.

(E. N. Taylor)

The "Ashleigh" (2) of 1925 laid up at Fowey, September 1933. (Tom Rayner)

The "Iddesleigh" (2) of 1927 was built for the Tatem Steam Navigation Co. Ltd. (Tom Rayner)

The "Winkleigh" (1) of 1927.

(E. N. Taylor)

The "Umberleigh" was a product in 1927 of William Gray and Co. Ltd., West Hartlepool. (Welsh Industrial & Maritime Museum).

The "Monkleigh" of 1927.

(Welsh Industrial & Maritime Museum).

The "Goodleigh" (1) laid up at Fowey in 1933. She was owned by a single-ship company, the Dulverton Steamship Co. Ltd.
(E. N. Taylor)

The "Filleigh" (1) was built in 1928 by Wm. Pickersgill and Sons Ltd., Sunderland for the Atlantic Shipping and Trading Co. Ltd.
(Tom Rayner)

The Appledore" was built in 1929 for G. C. Gibson's Maritime Shipping and Trading Co. Ltd.
(E. N. Taylor)

The "Everleigh" of 1930. (Tom Rayner)

The "Hadleigh" of 1930 laden with timber at Cardiff in 1936. (Welsh Industrial & Maritime Museum).

The "Hadleigh". (E. N. Taylor)

The "Northleigh" of 1937 seen with a timber cargo before the Second World War. (Tom Rayner)

A post-war view of the "Northleigh" at Cardiff.

(Welsh Industrial & Maritime Museum).

Another view of the "Northleigh". (Skyfotos Ltd.)

The "Winkleigh" (2) of 1940 in the English Channel. (Skyfotos Ltd.)

The "Winkleigh".

(Welsh Industrial & Maritime Museum).

The fifth "Chulmleigh" was a product of William Doxford and Sons Ltd., Sunderland. (Skyfotos Ltd.)

The Motorship "Chulmleigh" (5). (Welsh Industrial & Maritime Museum).

The turbine steamer "Lord Glanely" at Cardiff in 1948.

(Welsh Industrial & Maritime Museum).

The "Lord Glanely" was delivered by Wm. Pickersgill and Sons Ltd., Sunderland. (Welsh Industrial & Maritime Museum).

The "Lord Glanely" in the English Channel. (Skyfotos Ltd.)

At 8,261 gross tons, the "Glanely" built by Austin & Pickersgill Ltd., Sunderland, in 1960 was the largest ship to be owned by Tatems. (Skyfotos Ltd.)

The "Landwade" of 1961. (Skyfotos Ltd.)

Built in 1965 the motorship "Exning" was the last vessel to enter the Tatem fleet.

(Skyfotos Ltd.)

9. THE SPANISH CIVIL WAR

The Spanish Civil War had broken out on July 18, 1936 when the majority of the Armed Forces aided by the right wing of Spanish politics set about overthrowing the lawfully elected Popular Front or Republican Government. Within a month half of Spain was in the hands of troops under the control of General Franco. Initially he marched on Madrid, but had little success in taking the capital, thereafter he set about capturing the North of the country, and following his occupation of Bilbao on June 19, 1937 set about capturing the remainder of the North which was still in the hands of the Basques and Republicans, namely from Aviles in the West to Santander in the East.

The Northern ports were at that time blockaded by Franco's Nationalist Navy. As the Army marched on Santander following the fall of Bilbao they carried before them a human tide of refugees many of whom were fleeing from certain death at the hands of Franco's troops. This resulted in an influx into Santander and other Republican held ports of thousands of unfortunate souls who placed great strain on the already low food supplies. The Republicans had chartered a number of British owned ships to take food into the North and to bring out cargoes of refugees destined for French Bay of Biscay ports where they were sympathetically received. However, there was considerable risk involved as the Nationalist cruiser *Almirante Cervera* was in attendance with other units of the Navy. A number of ships had been damaged, captured and sunk as they entered the three mile limit off the North. It was only a matter of time before the territory fell, but meantime people were starving and there was great suffering. In Britain there was public outrage, and various committees were set up to send relief or to receive refugees.

Support in Wales for the Basque people had been magnificent. A Cardiff Committee of the National Joint Committee for Spanish Relief was established to maintain fifty Basque children at Cambria House, Caerleon, Monmouthshire. This home opened on July 10, 1937 and was supported by such influential persons as Lloyd George, Professor H. A. Marquand, the Archbishop of Wales and the Lord Mayor of Cardiff. Lord Glanely was a major supporter of the scheme.

Lord Glanely, apart from his support in South Wales, on learning of the plight of the people of Northern Spain, had allowed the Basques to charter his two oldest ships, the *Molton* and *Pilton*, to carry refugees from Northern Spain.

H.M.S. *Royal Oak* was in attendance off Santander in early July, 1937 to ensure that the Nationalist Navy did not interfere with British Merchantmen outside Spanish Territorial Waters, but was powerless to intervene within the three mile limit. On July 11 she observed three Welsh owned ships waiting their chance to enter Santander, these included the *Kenfig Pool* (Alfred Pope of Porthcawl), *Sarastone* (Stone and Rolfe, Llanelly) and Lord Glanely's *Molton* which was in ballast, and commanded by Captain R. H. Stears. The three ships remained outside the three mile limit hoping for the Nationalist cruiser, which had a long coastline to patrol, to pass out of sight long enough for them to dash into port.

On the morning of July 14 the *Molton* entered the three mile limit off Santander and was captured by the cruiser *Almirante Cervera* within sight of H.M.S. *Royal Oak* which in view of the merchant ship's position was powerless to intervene.

On July 15 Lieut. Colonel J. J. Llewellyn, Civil Lord of the Admiralty, in reply to a question in the House of Commons concerning the capture of the *Molton* said:

> According to a report which I have received from the Rear-Admiral, Second Battle Squadron, who was present in H.M.S. *Royal Oak*, the steamer *Molton* entered Spanish territorial waters opposite Santander at approximately 5.45 am yesterday. At this time the Spanish cruiser *Almirante Cervera* was outside territorial waters. When the *Molton* was some distance inside territorial waters the *Almirante Cervera* signalled to her, but these signals could not be distinguished from H.M.S. *Royal Oak*. Subsequently the *Almirante Cervera* fired two warning shots, after the second of which the *Molton* submitted, indicating the fact by altering course and reversing engines. The *Almirante Cervera* ordered the *Molton* to proceed on a Northerly course. Shortly afterwards the *Almirante Cervera* fired another warning shot, whereupon H.M.S. *Royal Oak* intervened and asked why she continued to fire after the ship had submitted. The *Almirante Cervera* replied that she fired because the *Molton* was delaying in carrying out the order. Thereafter the *Molton* steered the course ordered and was taken off under charge of the *Almirante Cervera*. I regret that I am not aware of her present whereabouts. The report I have received so far does not show that any signals were exchanged between the *Molton* and H.M.S. *Royal Oak* during the incident.

The *Molton* was actually taken to Bilbao, and was escorted there by the armed trawler *Galerna*. A complication at the time of the capture of the *Molton* which took some of the British warships attention was that at the moment that the *Molton* was entering the three mile limit, Jack Billmeir's steamer *Stanhill* decided to leave port with a full complement of refugees, and successfully made it out into international waters. There was uproar in the British Press, where it was not understood, or they did not want to understand how and why a British man-of-war was powerless to protect a British merchantman whilst in the territorial waters of another

Sovereign State. On July 19 Anthony Eden, the Foreign Secretary, made the following statement regarding the *Molton*, in the House of Commons:

> I understand that the steamer *Molton* was chartered on July 1 by the Basque Government agent in London for the purpose of evacuating civilian refugees from Northern Spain to French ports. Instructions have been sent to H.M. Ambassador at Hendaye to demand the release of the vessel and of her crew and to state that His Majesty's Government must hold General Franco's Government responsible for any injury or damage she may have incurred. It is reported in the Press that the ship is about to be released. I have not been able to confirm this.

Meanwhile the *Pilton* had actually succeeded in taking a cargo of coal, salt fish and two hundred motor cycles into Santander. Her Chief Engineer, William Patton, gave the following account of the ship's entry into port in his book *The Scrap Log of an Engineer*:

> The steamer *Pilton*, on which I was serving as Chief Engineer, was about five miles from the port of Santander when a British cruiser detached itself from a number of merchantmen, and made straight for our ship. Her commander hailed us by megaphone:
>
> "What ship?" he enquired.
>
> "The *Pilton* of London," replied our captain.
>
> "Where are you bound for?"
>
> "Santander."
>
> "What is your cargo?"
>
> "Coal and salt fish, with two hundred motor cycles."
>
> "Have you a non-intervention officer on board?"
>
> "Yes."
>
> "We strongly advise you not to enter the port."
>
> Our captain decided to explore the situation further. Ahead was a long line of British ships riding on the three mile limit; we steamed up to them, then stopped engines. Between the ships and shore, Franco's cruiser, the *Almirante Cervera*, moved about waiting for the chance to pounce upon any ship that got within the three mile limit. The distant rumble of gunfire could be heard coming from over the range of mountains where Franco's army, after capturing Bilbao, was pressing on to Santander. Naval advice could not very well be ignored, but we had brought our cargo all the way from England, and our instructions were to deliver it to the Spanish Government forces in Santander.
>
> In face of the uncertainty of the situation, our captain sent a radio message to the owners of the vessel in Cardiff for further instructions. The reply was contradictory: "Proceed to port. Follow advice of Senior Naval Officer." While hesitating what to do next, he received

the following message from the Captain of the Port, Santander: "British naval advice is general, and given to all ships. We guarantee protection. The port is quiet."

Our captain hesitated no longer, and he informed the British Naval officer of his intention to attempt to enter port.

"You do so at your own risk," came the reply.

Running the blockade depended upon seizing the opportunity when it arose. The *Almirante Cervera* covered about forty miles of seacoast, guarding the entrances not only of Santander but also those of Gijon and Aviles, and on her patrols she was frequently out of sight, though she had a disconcerting habit of doubling back on her course.

The cruiser could not guard three ports at the same time, however, and the chances of escaping her attentions looked good. At dawn the next day then, with a full head of steam and no sign of the warship, the *Pilton* and two other ships made a successful dash into port.

The full text of this account appears in my book—*Welsh Blockade Runners in the Spanish Civil War* (1985). The ship actually left Santander with 2,500 refugees, mainly women and children, and took them across the Bay of Biscay to St. Nazaire. Following this voyage the *Pilton* dashed into Aviles on July 27, 1937 and subsequently carried another batch of refugees out to France. Having done more than most Lord Glanely decided to withdraw the ship from the trade, particularly after the French Government declared an unwillingness to take further Spanish refugees.

Meanwhile the *Molton* was still held at Bilbao together with her crew. Repeated representations from the British Government eventually secured the vessel's release and on September 10 she was allowed to leave Spanish waters. She made for Bordeaux where Captain Stear communicated with the Cardiff office. Lord Glanely was relieved to hear of the safe return of the ship, but the decision to withdraw from the trade had already been made. The war in the North of Spain came to an end on October 21, 1937 when the last pockets of resistance fell.

10. THE LATE 1930s

Total tonnage handled at Cardiff during the 1930s tended to be in the region of half that handled during 1913. There had been a few better years in the early 1920s and a slight recovery at the end of that decade. However, it was clear to Lord Glanely that the prosperity of his business was less than ever linked to the coal trade. His ships were still carrying their share of this trade, but more and more were being fixed on charters in the worldwide tramp trades. He had, in common with Reardon Smith, established important links with the West Coast of North America, and was lifting regular cargoes of grain and lumber from this region.

In the development of the ports of South Wales, shipowners had tended to standardise their fleets on two trades; vessels in the region of 4,500 tons deadweight for the Baltic and Mediterranean, and 7,000 to 8,000 tonners for the longer voyages including the River Plate trade. Lord Glanely had operated ships of both sizes, and had been engaged in both the intermediate and general tramp trades. However, in the late 1930s he made the decision to concentrate on the longer voyages and in consequence disposed of his smaller ships. This had been started with the sale of the *Goodleigh* (1) in 1937. As a result, in 1938 he disposed of the *Molton* and *Pilton* for further trading. These ships had given almost twenty years service in the fleet, and were to be lost in the Second World War.

Such had been the improvement in prospects by 1936 that Lord Glanely decided to enlarge the fleet by building a number of ships in the region of 10,000 tons deadweight for the general tramp trades. These ships were not all ordered at the same time, but tended to be ordered in groups. Lord Glanely placed orders for three ships with Wm. Pickersgill and Sons Ltd., Sunderland, all of which were to be coal-burning steamers. However, he decided to order a single motor vessel from William Doxford and Sons Ltd., Sunderland, being the first such vessel to join the fleet. South Wales tramp shipowners had traditionally kept to steamships because of the wealth of good quality steam coal which was available. A steamship was also considerably cheaper to build. The ordering of this motorship was therefore a quite radical move, and was undertaken in order to assess the future of this form of propulsion in the fleet for the future. The ship was duly completed in 1938, and was named *Lady Glanely* in memory of the founder's wife who had tragically died in a road accident at Newmarket in 1930. The three steamers were completed at Pickersgill's as the *Northleigh*, *Chulmleigh* (4) and *Goodleigh* (2) and had been built one after the other on their East Berth. Subsequently a fourth ship was ordered from Pickersgill's which was finally delivered in 1940.

The following table gives details of the progress of the four steamers during construction at Pickersgill's:

Yard No.	237	238	240	242
Name	Northleigh	Chulmleigh	Goodleigh	Winkleigh
Keel Laid	22.12.36	12.6.37	28.12.37	6.5.39
Commenced Framing	18.2.37	28.7.37	22.2.38	11.10.39
Framed	24.3.37	31.8.37	30.3.38	15.11.39
Commenced Plating	1.3.37	18.8.37	28.2.38	—
Plated	20.5.37	3.11.37	18.5.38	—
Launched	10.6.37	18.12.37	28.7.38	24.2.40
Went for Engines	30.7.37	20.12.37	4.8.38	24.2.40
Returned from Engineers	—	27.1.38	12.9.38	—
Completed	10.9.37	4.3.38	10.9.38	1.5.40
Trial Trip	12.9.37	7.5.38	6.10.38	—

As can be seen the *Northleigh* was launched on June 10, 1937 and the keel of the *Chulmleigh* was laid on the same slipway two days later. The *Chulmleigh* was launched on December 18, 1937 and the keel of the *Goodleigh* was again laid on the same slipway but ten days later. In relation to the *Winkleigh* she was not ordered until well after the other three had been completed and been in service for some time. The yard had actually been without a ship under construction for a short period. Ship No. 239 was a steamer for Headlam and Son of Whitby, whilst Ship No. 241 was the *Daydawn* for Claymore Shipping Co. Ltd., of Cardiff. Both of these ships had been built on the West Berth at the yard.

The *Lady Glanely* and *Chulmleigh* were both completed in May, 1938, and there was much publicity when it was announced that both ships were to cover the same ports on their respective maiden voyages, particularly when one notes that one was a motor vessel and the other a steamship. Lord Glanely gained much valuable data on the merits of oil and coal from the results of the voyages, which were in ballast from Sunderland to Galveston in the Gulf of Mexico where they loaded malt grain for the United Kingdom.

With the delivery of these ships the fleet comprised the following vessels:

Name	Year Built	Gross Tons
Iddesleigh (2)	1927	5,205
Winkleigh (1)	1927	5,055
Umberleigh	1927	4,950
Monkleigh	1927	5,203
Filleigh (1)	1928	4,856
Everleigh	1930	5,222
Hadleigh	1930	5,222
Northleigh	1937	5,450
Chulmleigh (4)	1938	5,445

Name	Year Built	Gross Tons
Lady Glanely	1938	5,497
Goodleigh (2)	1938	5,448
Winkleigh (2)	1940	5,468

The *Winkleigh* (2) was named after the ship of that name which was lost by enemy action in 1939.

11. THE SECOND WORLD WAR

At the outbreak of the Second World War on September 3, 1939 Lord Glanely was operating a fine fleet of eleven vessels with a further one in the course of construction. Of these eight were to be lost during the period of hostilities, seven through enemy action and one through marine hazard. In addition a vessel managed on behalf of the British Government was also lost by enemy action.

The first loss was the *Winkleigh* (1) which was torpedoed and sunk by the German submarine *U48* on September 8, 1939, just five days after the declaration of war. She had been on passage from Vancouver to Manchester with a cargo of lumber and grain at the time of the sinking. On December 2, 1940 the firm was unfortunate to lose two ships on the same day and from the same Eastbound convoy, HX90. The motorship *Lady Glanely* (Vancouver for London) was torpedoed and sunk by the submarine *U101* whilst the *Goodleigh* (2) fell victim to a torpedo from *U52*.

Having moved temporarily to Weston-super-Mare, Lord Glanely was tragically killed when the town was bombed by enemy aircraft on June 24, 1942. He had achieved outstanding success as a shipowner but is remembered more for his many public benefactions and for his love of racehorses. He was succeeded as Chairman of the group of companies and principal shareholder in W. J. Tatem Ltd. by his nephew, Mr. G. C. Gibson, who at this time disposed of the Maritime Shipping and Trading Co. Ltd., and its single ship the *Appledore* to Michalinos and Co. Ltd.

On October 17, 1942 the *Empire Chaucer*, which was managed by W. J. Tatem Ltd. on behalf of the Ministry of War Transport, was torpedoed and sunk by the submarine *U504* South West of Cape Agulhas. This ship was only five months old, having been completed in May, 1942 by Wm. Pickersgill and Sons Ltd., Sunderland.

On November 5, 1942 the *Chulmleigh* (4) was wrecked when she struck a reef and capsized off South Cape, Spitzbergen whilst on passage from the United Kingdom to the Russian port of Archangel with urgently needed war supplies. Five months later on March 16, 1943 the *Hadleigh* was torpedoed and sunk by the submarine *U77* in the Mediterranean, North West of Oran. On August 17, 1944, whilst acting as a supply vessel at the Normany Beach-head, the *Iddesleigh* (2) was torpedoed and sunk by a one man torpedo.

The *Everleigh* was torpedoed and sunk in the English Channel, whilst on passage London to New York by *U101* on February 6, 1945, and on April 18, 1945 of the same year the final war loss occurred when the *Filleigh* was torpedoed and sunk by *U245* in the North Sea, whilst on passage from London to Antwerp. This was a particularly unfortunate casualty, as only two further British vessels were lost after this before the end of hostilities.

As with the First World War, the casualties amongst the company's personnel during this second conflict were tragically high, and many acts of heroism were recorded and recognised with the presentation of awards.

Apart from the *Empire Chaucer* previously noted as a war loss, the firm also managed three other vessels on behalf of the Ministry of War Transport, the Danish *Kirsten Maersk* (1940-1942), *Empire Service* (1943-1945) and the *Empire Tudor* (1944-1946).

At the conclusion of hostilities the fleet had been reduced to the following four ships:—

Name	Year Built	Gross Tons
Umberleigh	1927	4,950
Monkleigh	1927	5,203
Northleigh	1937	5,450
Winkleigh (2)	1940	5,468

12. THE POST-WAR YEARS

George Gibson was no stranger to the business of ship management. He had been involved in the firm at Cardiff since way back in 1912 and had been a shipowner in his own right since 1919. In the 1930s he had largely taken over responsibility for the day to day management of the business, and was therefore well placed to run the firm.

At the end of the war he set about trading the surviving four ships, two of which were owned by W. J. Tatem Ltd., and one each by the Tatem Steam Navigation Co. Ltd. and the Atlantic Shipping and Trading Co. Ltd. Coal shipments were never again to hold the important position they had held in the past, and much of the freights undertaken were in trades much further afield. Although the North American Pacific Coast continued to yield some useful charters, the ships were now to be seen in all parts of the world.

With the shortage of tonnage available after the war the freight market was temporarily very high, and the price being paid for quite old vessels was very good. In consequence it was decided to dispose of the two older ships whilst the demand was at its height. In this way the *Umberleigh* which was sold in 1946 and the *Monkleigh* which followed a year later, almost provided the means for the acquisition of two new ships. The vessels acquired were the motorship *Chulmleigh* (5) from William Doxford and Sons Ltd., Sunderland which was delivered in 1946. This ship had been ordered by the Ministry of War Transport and was completed for Tatems. The other ship was the turbine steamer *Lord Glanely* constructed by Wm. Pickersgill and Sons Ltd., Sunderland, to the company's own order.

In view of the fact that the coal trade from South Wales had all but ended and the generally poor returns from shipowning it was not thought wise or prudent to build the fleet up to its previous size. Much of the assets of W. J. Tatem Ltd. and the companies under its management, had for many years been in investments completely unrelated to the shipping industry.

Returning to the construction of the turbine steamer *Lord Glanely* at Pickersgill's the following details relate to her building:—

Yard No. 304

Lord Glanely

Constructed at West Yard No. 4 Berth

25. 6.1946	Keel laid
	Commenced framing
5.10.1946	Framed
	Commenced plating
18. 1.1947	Plated
6. 3.1947	Launched
	Grounded at Shorts Quay
11. 3.1947	Drydocked for repairs
12. 3.1947	Undocked
14. 4.1947	Went to Engineers (boilers)
24. 4.1947	Returned from Engineers
10. 6.1947	Completed
10. 6.1947	Trials commenced
	Returned to yard, turbine trouble
12. 6.1947	Trial Trip.

As can be seen the ship grounded at Short's Quay on March 6, 1947. This related to the actual launch of the vessel. Having gone down the slip she eluded her tugs and ran stern first into the opposite bank where she received slight damage to her rudder which necessitated drydocking for twenty four hours.

For the next ten years the fleet was maintained at four vessels and in April, 1957 George Gibson was joined by one of his sons, Major William David Gibson, who joined the business following a career in the Welsh Guards. After the Second World War the ships were all registered in the ownership of the public company, the Atlantic Shipping and Trading Co. Ltd., or the private family company, W. J. Tatem Ltd., although all were actually managed by the latter company. Eventually with the demise of the coal trade the Cardiff office was closed and in 1960 the firm's offices were moved from 7, St. Helen's Place, London to Forum House, 15/18, Lime Street, London.

In 1956 the *Northleigh* was disposed of and was replaced during 1957 with the newbuilding *Filleigh* (2), a motor vessel from Bartram and Sons Ltd., Sunderland. In 1960 two ships, the *Winkleigh* (2) and *Lord Glanely* were sold followed the next year by the *Chulmleigh* (5). However two ships joined the fleet when the *Glanely* and the *Landwade* were delivered from the Sunderland yards of Austin & Pickersgill Ltd. and Bartram and Sons Ltd., respectively.

At this time all three ships were registered in the ownership of the Atlantic Shipping and Trading Co. Ltd., which at that time had an authorised share capital of £2million of which only £1million was issued.

The company was rich in assets and reserves, and had the following directors:—

G. C. Gibson, Chairman
Sir J. E. A. Baldwin, KBE, DSO, DL, JP
Sir Leighton Seager, BT, CBE, DL, JP
Kenneth Thomas
J. H. Tonge, also Company Secretary
Major W. D. Gibson

The firm of W. J. Tatem Ltd. which was a closed company and which was still responsible for the management of the ships was directed by George Gibson and his family, there being no outside directors or shareholders.

The principal shareholders in the Atlantic Shipping and Trading Co. Ltd. were as follows:—

Name	Holding—£
Branch Nominees Ltd., London	283,697
Mrs. Florence May Cox & Cecil Henry Cox, Newport, jointly	8,231
Cyril Davies Gething, Bournemouth	7,690
George Cock Gibson, Cardiff Docks	221,556
George Simon Cecil Gibson, Newmarket	11,408
William David Gibson, Newmarket	20,246
W. D. Gibson and G. S. C. Gibson, Newmarket, jointly	5,425
Lloyds Bank (Cardiff) Nominees Ltd., Cardiff	4,895
Charles Henry March, George Frederick Kenneth Morgan and George Cock Gibson, Cardiff, jointly	59,282
National Provincial Bank Ltd., London	63,283
National Provincial Bank Ltd., (G. C. Gibson), London	98,269

With the fall in freight rates in the early 1960s the fleet was reduced to two ships with the sale of the six year old *Filleigh* (2), in 1963 for further trading. By 1965 conditions had improved sufficiently to justify the arrival of a third vessel, the *Exning*, from Austin & Pickersgill Ltd. The *Landwade* and *Exning* took their names from Mr. G. C. Gibson's home which is still at Landwade Hall, Exning, Newmarket. During 1969 the *Glanely* was sold and for three years the remaining two ships continued trading. In 1972, however, the *Landwade* was disposed of and this was followed in 1973 with the sale of the *Exning*.

The decision was taken to withdraw from shipowning altogether as in a highly cyclical industry the rewards were completely out of proportion to the capital employed and in consequence the Atlantic Shipping and

Trading Co. Ltd. was disposed of. Today the firm of W. J. Tatem Ltd. is a highly successful investment company under the directions of Major William David Gibson (Chairman), his brother George Simon Cecil Gibson, DL, JP, (who is also the company secretary), and a fourth generation of the family—Martin George Simon Gibson and John Homfray.

The firm has moved back to Cardiff recently, and its registered address is at Baltic House, Mount Stuart Square, a fitting home for such an old established business.

APPENDICES

13. APPENDIX ONE
FLEET LIST

Name and Period in Fleet	Gross Tons	History
Lady Lewis (1) 1897-1906	2,950	1897 built by Richardson, Duck & Company, Stockton on Tees as *Lady Lewis* for the Lady Lewis Steamship Co. Ltd. (W. J. Tatem and Company); 3.4.1906 wrecked near Mogotes Point, Argentina, whilst on a voyage from Bahia Blanca to Barcelona with a cargo of wheat and maize.
Sir W. T. Lewis 1898-1913	3,517	1898 built by Richardson, Duck and Company, Stockton on Tees as *Sir W. T. Lewis* for the Sir W. T. Lewis Steamship Co. Ltd. (W. J. Tatem and Company); 1910 transferred to the Tatem Steam Navigation Co. Ltd. (W. J. Tatem and Company); 1913 to E. C. Embiricos (J. D. Corcodilos), Greece, renamed *Nea Ellas*; 1915 to J. D. Corcodilos, Greece; 1923 to G. N. Embiricos, Greece, renamed *Eugena Cambanis*; 29.11.1940 reported in distress in position 46.53'N, 48.37'W, whilst on a voyage to Belfast and presumed to have foundered in a gale.
Shandon (1) 1899-1910	3,850	1899 built by Richardson, Duck and Company, Stockton on Tees as *Shandon* for the Shandon Steamship Co. Ltd. (W. J. Tatem and Company); 29.12.1909 stranded 1½ miles S.E. of Heligoland whilst on a voyage from Odessa to the River Weser; 1910 refloated and sold to H. Neugebauer and Company, Germany; 1911 to Menzell-Linie G.m.b.H., Germany, renamed *Hedwig Menzell*; 1912 to Vulkan Reederei Dampfer Franz Wilke G.m.b.H. (N. V. Handels en Transport Maats Vulcaan), Germany, renamed *Franz Wilke*; 1919 surrendered as a prize to Great Britain and allocated to the Shipping Controller, managers—W. Runciman and Co. Ltd.; 1921 to Amelia Steamship Co. Ltd., Newcastle upon Tyne, renamed *Mary Amelia*; 1923 management passed to Logothettis

Name and Period in Fleet	Gross Tons	History
		and Weston, London; 1925 to Essex Transport and Trading Co. Ltd. (Meldrum and Swinson), London, renamed *Essex Heath*; 1930 broken up at Rotterdam by G. B. Pas and Sons.
Chulmleigh (1) 1900-1915	3,997	1900 built by Richardson, Duck and Company, Stockton on Tees as *Chulmleigh* for the Chulmleigh Steamship Co. Ltd. (W. J. Tatem and Company); 1910 transferred to the Tatem Steam Navigation Co. Ltd. (W. J. Tatem and Company); 1915 to Brys and Gylsen Ltd., London, renamed *Bretanier*; 1918 owners restyled as Lloyd Royal Belge (Great Britain) Ltd., London; 1923 to "Nova Genuensis" Soc. Anon. per l'Industria ed il Commercio Marit, Italy, renamed *Fidelitas*; 1926 to Levante Soc di Nav. a Vap, Yugoslavia, renamed *Drina*; 26.1.1931 wrecked on Pearl Rock whilst on a voyage from Fellonica to Amsterdam with a cargo of pyrites.
Southport 1900-1912	3,588	1900 built by Richardson, Duck and Company, Stockton on Tees as *Southport* for the Southport Steamship Co. Ltd. (W. J. Tatem and Company); 1910 transferred to the Tatem Steam Navigation Co. Ltd. (W. J. Tatem and Company); 1912 to Lewis Trading Co. Ltd. (T. Lewis), Cardiff; 4.9.1914 captured by the German cruiser *Geier* off the Caroline Islands; the engines were immobilized by the raider whilst other shipping was pursued. The crew succeeded in repairing the engine and on 30.9.1914 arrived at Brisbane; 1916 to Sefton Steamship Co. Ltd. (H. E. Moss and Company), Liverpool; 1923 to G. F. Andreadis, Greece, renamed *Tithis*; 1932 broken up in Italy.
Westward Ho 1900-1913	3,596	1900 built by Richardson, Duck and Company, Stockton on Tees as *Westward Ho* for the Westward Ho Steamship Co. Ltd. (W. J. Tatem and Company); 1910 transferred to the Tatem Steam Navigation Co. Ltd. (W. J. Tatem and Company); 1913 to Lewis Maritime Co. Ltd. (T. Lewis), Cardiff; 1916 to the Bay Steamship Co.

Name and Period in Fleet	Gross Tons	History

Ltd., London, renamed *Baywest*; 9.9.1918 struck by a shell from a French steamer 1½ miles W. by S. from the Longships, Cornwall, whilst on a voyage from Fort de France to Marseilles; she caught fire and sank as a derelict.

Wooda 1901-1915 — 3,804 — 1901 built by Richardson, Duck and Company, Stockton on Tees as *Wooda* for the Wooda Steamship Co. Ltd. (W. J. Tatem and Company); 1910 transferred to the Tatem Steam Navigation Co. Ltd. (W. J. Tatem and Company); 1915 to Brys and Gylsen Ltd., London, renamed *Morinier*; 1918 owners restyled as Lloyd Royal Belge (Great Britain) Ltd., London; 1922 to Unione Soc. Anon, di Nav., Italy, renamed *Uguaglianza*; 1929 to Cigini G. and F. Gazzolo, Italy, renamed *Nervi*; 30.6.1931 sank 20 miles North of Cape Ivi, Algeria after stranding near Tenes whilst on a voyage from La Goulette to Dunkirk with a cargo of iron ore.

Chorley 1901-1916 — 3,828 — 1901 built by Richardson, Duck and Company, Stockton on Tees as *Chorley* for the Chorley Steamship Co. Ltd. (W. J. Tatem and Company); 1910 transferred to the Tatem Steam Navigation Co. Ltd. (W. J. Tatem and Company); 1916 to Brys and Gylsen Ltd., London; 22.3.1917 torpedoed and sunk 25 miles E. by S. of Start Point by the German submarine *UC48*.

Appledore (1) 1901-1917 — 3,843 — 1901 built by Richardson, Duck and Company, Stockton on Tees as *Appledore* for the Appledore Steamship Co. Ltd. (W. J. Tatem and Company); 1910 transferred to the Tatem Steam Navigation Co. Ltd. (W. J. Tatem and Company); 9.6.1917 torpedoed and sunk 164 miles S. by W. from Fastnet by the German submarine *U70*.

Torridge (1) 1901-1910 — 3,838 — 1902 built by Richardson, Duck and Company, Stockton on Tees as *Torridge* for the Torridge Steamship Co. Ltd. (W. J. Tatem and Company); 1910 transferred to the Tatem Steam Navigation

Name and Period in Fleet	Gross Tons	History
		Co. Ltd. (W. J. Tatem and Company); 18.4.1910 wrecked on Farquhar Island whilst on a voyage from Port Natal to Galle in ballast.
Northam 1902-1915	3,842	1902 built by Richardson, Duck and Company, Stockton on Tees as *Northam* for the Northam Steamship Co. Ltd. (W. J. Tatem and Company); 1910 transferred to the Tatem Steam Navigation Co. Ltd. (W. J. Tatem and Company); 1915 to F. W. Lund and W. H. Dixon (Harris and Dixon), London; 1916 to Brys and Gylsen Ltd., London, renamed *Normandier*; 1918 owners restyled as Lloyd Royal Belge (Great Britain) Ltd., London; 1922 to Bristol Channel Steamers Ltd. (J. German and Company), Cardiff, renamed *Holms Light*; 1926 management transferred to Lewis Lougher and Co. Ltd., Cardiff; 1926 to Lewis Steamship Co. Ltd. (T. Lewis), Cardiff, renamed *Portishead*; 1927 management transferred to S. Lewis; 1931 to Italian owners, renamed *Quadrifoglio*; 12.1931 broken up in Italy.
Dunster 1902-1915	4,662	1902 built by Richardson, Duck and Company, Stockton on Tees as *Dunster* for the Dunster Steamship Co. Ltd. (W. J. Tatem and Company); 1910 transferred to the Tatem Steam Navigation Co. Ltd. (W. J. Tatem and Company); 1915 to Brys and Gylsen Ltd., London, renamed *Suevier*; 15.2.1916 abandoned on fire in position 39.01'N, 67.00'W, following an explosion amongst cylinders of chlorine gas whilst on a voyage from New York to Havre with general cargo.
Dulverton 1904-1907	4,508	1904 built by Richardson, Duck and Company, Stockton on Tees as *Dulverton* for the Dulverton Steamship Co. Ltd. (W. J. Tatem and Company); 13.4.1907 sailed from Bahia Blanca bound for Antwerp with a cargo of wheat and disappeared; she was last seen on 15.4.1907, by the Cardiff steamer *Lesreaulx*, and at that time was stopped with engine trouble, and refused an offer of assistance.

Name and Period in Fleet	Gross Tons	History
Iddesleigh (1) 1904-1919	4,027	1904 built by Richardson, Duck and Company, Stockton on Tees as *Iddesleigh* for the Iddesleigh Steamship Co. Ltd. (W. J. Tatem and Company); 1910 transferred to the Tatem Steam Navigation Co. Ltd. (W. J. Tatem and Company); 1917 transferred to the Atlantic Shipping and Trading Co. Ltd. (W. J. Tatem Ltd.); 1919 to Mediterranean Cargo Steamers Ltd. (W. J. Foster), London; 1922 to Soc. Anon. Ilva (Lloyd Mediterraneo), Italy; 1923 to Lloyd Mediterraneo, Italy, renamed *Valnoce*; 1926 to 'Corrado' Soc. Anon. di Nav., Italy, renamed *Caterina Madre*; 13.9.1943 struck a mine and sank 10 miles off the island of S. Andrea, near Gallipoli.
Wellington 1905-1918	5,600	1905 built by William Doxford and Sons Ltd., Sunderland as *Wellington* for the Wellington Steamship Co. Ltd. (W. J. Tatem and Company); 1910 transferred to the Tatem Steam Navigation Co. Ltd. (W. J. Tatem and Company); 1917 transferred to the Atlantic Shipping and Trading Co. Ltd. (W. J. Tatem Ltd.); 16.9.1918 torpedoed and sunk 175 miles N. by W. from Cape Villano by the German submarine *U118*.
Torrington 1905-1917	5,597	1905 built by William Doxford and Sons Ltd., Sunderland as *Torrington* for the Torrington Steamship Co. Ltd. (W. J. Tatem and Company); 1910 transferred to the Tatem Steam Navigation Co. Ltd. (W. J. Tatem and Company); 8.4.1917 torpedoed and sunk 150 miles S.W. of the Scilly Isles by the German submarine *U55*.
Lady Lewis (2) 1907-1911	3,477	1907 built by Richardson, Duck and Company, Stockton on Tees as *Lady Lewis* for the Lady Lewis Steamship Co. Ltd. (W. J. Tatem and Company); 1910 transferred to the Tatem Steam Navigation Co. Ltd. (W. J. Tatem and Company); 1911 to Adelaide Steamship Co. Ltd., Adelaide, renamed *Yankalilla*; 1929 to Rederi A/B Ovidia (C. I. Morin), Sweden, renamed *Bolivia*; 1931 to

Name and Period in Fleet	Gross Tons	History
		Rederi A/B Iris (C. Abrahamsen), Sweden, renamed *Pluto*; 1933 to Rederi A/B Pluto (E. Erikson), Finland; 28.6.1941 torpedoed and sunk 100 miles N.N.W. of the Butt of Lewis by the German submarine *U146*.
Cloutsham 1910-1919	4,907	1910 built by William Doxford and Sons Ltd., Sunderland, as *Cloutsham* for the Tatem Steam Navigation Co. Ltd. (W. J. Tatem and Company); 1917 transferred to the Atlantic Shipping and Trading Co. Ltd. (W. J. Tatem Ltd.); 1919 to Mediterranean Cargo Steamers Ltd. (W. J. Foster), London; 1922 to Soc. Anon Ilva (Lloyd Mediterraneo), Italy; 1923 to Soc. Italiana di Nav. (Lloyd Mediterraneo), Italy, renamed *Vallescura*; 1926 to Lloyd Mediterraneo, Italy; 1935 to I.N.S.A. (Industrie Navali Soc. Anon.), Italy, renamed *Fedora*; 1938 to Giovanni Gavarone, Italy; 10.1.1942 torpedoed and sunk off Cape Dukato by H.M.S. *Thrasher*.
Quantock 1910-1919	4,470	1910 built by William Doxford and Sons Ltd., Sunderland, as *Quantock* for the Tatem Steam Navigation Co. Ltd. (W. J. Tatem and Company); 1917 transferred to the Atlantic Shipping and Trading Co. Ltd. (W. J. Tatem Ltd.); 1919 to Mediterranean Cargo Steamers Ltd. (W. J. Foster), London; 1922 to Soc. Anon. Ilva (Lloyd Mediterraneo), Italy; 1923 to Lloyd Mediterraneo, Italy, renamed *Valverde*; 1936 to I.N.S.A. (Indistrie Navali Soc. Anon.), Italy; 9.9.1943 sunk by German M.T.B.'s off Casteliogncello.
Bideford 1910-1919	3,562	1910 built by Craig, Taylor and Co. Ltd., Stockton on Tees as *Bideford* for the Tatem Steam Navigation Co. Ltd. (W. J. Tatem and Company); 1917 transferred to the Atlantic Shipping and Trading Co. Ltd. (W. J. Tatem Ltd.); 1919 to North Wales Shipping Co. Ltd. (H. Roberts and Son), Newcastle upon Tyne; 1921 to North Shipping Co. Ltd. (H. Roberts and Son), Newcastle upon Tyne,

Name and Period in Fleet	Gross Tons	History
		renamed *North Anglia*; 1933 to M. A. Embiricos, Greece, renamed *Corinthiakos*; 20.11.1942 torpedoed and sunk off Lourenco Marques in position 25.42′S, 33.27′E, by the German submarine *U181*.
Eggesford (1) 1910-1914	3,566	1910 built by Craig, Taylor and Co. Ltd., Stockton on Tees, as *Eggesford* for the Tatem Steam Navigation Co. Ltd. (W. J. Tatem and Company); 1914 to D. H. Stathatos, Greece, renamed *Maria Stathatos*; 1924 to Goulandris Bros., Greece, renamed *Ioannis P. Goulandris*; 1.12.1942 sank off New York following a collision with the Panamanian steamer *Intrepido*.
Bampton 1910-1919	4,496	1910 built by Richardson, Duck and Company, Stockton on Tees, as *Bampton* for the Tatem Steam Navigation Co. Ltd. (W. J. Tatem and Company); 1917 transferred to the Atlantic Shipping and Trading Co. Ltd. (W. J. Tatem Ltd.); 1919 to Mediterranean Cargo Steamers Ltd. (W. J. Foster), London; 1922 to Soc. Anon. Ilva (Lloyd Mediterraneo), Italy; 1923 to Lloyd Mediterraneo, Italy, renamed *Valrossa*; 1935 to Giuseppe Gavarone, Italy, renamed *Ninuccia*; 28.1.1942 torpedoed and sunk off Mulo Island by the British submarine H.M.S. *Thorn*.
Exford (1) *Brendon* 1911-1919	4,542	1911 built by Craig, Taylor and Co. Ltd., Stockton on Tees, as *Exford* for the Tatem Steam Navigation Co. Ltd. (W. J. Tatem and Company); 19.10.1914 captured by the German cruiser *Emden* in position 08.27′N, 74.49′E and released with a German prize crew on board; 11.12.1914 arrived at Singapore after being recaptured by H.M.S. *Empress of Asia*; 1915 returned to owners and renamed *Brendon*; 1917 transferred to the Atlantic Shipping and Trading Co. Ltd. (W. J. Tatem Ltd.); 1919 to Mediterranean Cargo Steamers Ltd. (W. J. Foster), London; 1922 to Soc. Anon. Ilva (Lloyd Mediterraneo), Italy; 1923 to Lloyd Mediterraneo,

Name and Period in Fleet	Gross Tons	History
		Italy, renamed *Valnegra*; 1934 to Fratelli Rizzuto, Italy, renamed *Assunzione*; 1951 renamed *Santa Elisabetta*; 1953 to Soc. Officina Malvicini Vapori, Italy; 1953 broken up at La Spezia.
Braunton 1911-1916	4,575	1911 built by Richardson, Duck and Company, Stockton on Tees as *Braunton* for the Tatem Steam Navigation Co. Ltd. (W. J. Tatem and Company); 7.4.1916 torpedoed and sunk 4½ miles off Beachy Head by the German submarine *UB 29* whilst on a voyage from Boulogne to Newport with a cargo of Government stores.
Torridge (2) 1912-1916	5,036	1912 built by Bartram and Sons Ltd., Sunderland, as *Torridge* for the Tatem Steam Navigation Co. Ltd. (W. J. Tatem and Company); 6.9.1916 captured by the German submarine *UB29* and sunk by bombs 40 miles S.S.W. of Start Point whilst on a voyage from Genoa to the River Tyne in ballast.
Exford (2) 1914-1917	4,503	1914 built by Bartram and Sons Ltd., Sunderland, as *Exford* for the Tatem Steam Navigation Co. Ltd. (W. J. Tatem Ltd.); she had originally been under construction as the *Salopian* for the Cambrian Steam Navigation Co. Ltd. (J. Mathias and Son), Cardiff, and was purchased whilst on the stocks; 14.7.1917 torpedoed and sunk 180 miles W. by S½S from Ushant by the German submarine *U48*.
Eggesford (2) 1914-1919	4,414	1914 built by R. Thompson and Sons Ltd., Sunderland, as *Eggesford* for the Tatem Steam Navigation Co. Ltd. (W. J. Tatem Ltd.); she had originally been under construction as the *Recina* for Societa in Azioni Ungaro Croata di Nav. Marittima a Vap., Austria, and had been seized as a prize on the stocks on 3.8.1914, and purchased by the company; 1917 transferred to the Atlantic Shipping and Trading Co. Ltd. (W. J. Tatem Ltd.); 1919 to Mediterranean Cargo Steamers Ltd. (W. J. Foster), London; 1922 to Soc. Anon. Ilva (Lloyd Mediterraneo), Italy; 1923 to Lloyd Mediterraneo, Italy,

Name and Period in Fleet	Gross Tons	History
		renamed *Valdirosa*; 1936 to I.N.S.A. (Industrie Navali Soc. Anon.), Italy; 9.1943 seized by German forces; 7.1944 scuttled at Leghorn, subsequently salved and broken up.
Honiton 1915	4,914	1915 built by A. McMillan and Son Ltd., Dumbarton, as *Honiton* for the Tatem Steam Navigation Co. Ltd. (W. J. Tatem Ltd.); 30.8.1915 mined 2½ miles E. of Longsand Light Vessel whilst on a voyage from Buenos Aires to Hull with a cargo of maize and linseed; beached at Shoeburyness and declared a total loss.
Chulmleigh (2) 1916-1917	4,911	1916 built by A. McMillan and Son Ltd., Dumbarton, as *Chulmleigh* for the Tatem Steam Navigation Co. Ltd. (W. J. Tatem Ltd.); 1917 transferred to the Atlantic Shipping and Trading Co. Ltd. (W. J. Tatem Ltd.); 14.9.1917 torpedoed and sunk 10 miles S.W. by W. of Cape Salou, Spain by the German submarine *U64*.
Ashleigh (1) 1917	6,985	1917 built by Ropner and Sons Ltd., Stockton on Tees, as *Ashleigh* for the Tatem Steam Navigation Co. Ltd. (W. J. Tatem Ltd.); 23.7.1917 torpedoed and sunk 290 miles S.W. of Fastnet by the German submarine *U54*.
Buckleigh (1) 1917-1919	4,920	1917 built by A. McMillan and Son Ltd., Dumbarton, as *Buckleigh* for the Atlantic Shipping and Trading Co. Ltd. (W. J. Tatem Ltd.); 1919 to Mediterranean Cargo Steamers Ltd. (W. J. Foster), London; 1922 to Soc. Anon. Ilva (Lloyd Mediterraneo), Italy; 1923 to Lloyd Mediterraneo, Italy, renamed *Valfiorita*; 1935 to I.N.S.A. (Industrie Navali Soc. Anon.), Italy, renamed *Delia*; 1938 to Giovanni Gavarone, Italy; 16.4.1942 torpedoed and sunk off Villanova, Brindisi.
Shandon (2) 1919-1934	3,069	1919 built by Irvine's Shipbuilding and Dry Dock Co. Ltd., West Hartlepool; Laid down as the *War Gale* for the Shipping Controller, but completed as

Name and Period in Fleet	Gross Tons	History
		the *Shandon* for the Tatem Steam Navigation Co. Ltd. (W. J. Tatem Ltd.); 1920 transferred to the Foreland Shipping and Trading Co. Ltd. (W. J. Tatem Ltd.); 1921 transferred to the Atlantic Shipping and Trading Co. Ltd. (W. J. Tatem Ltd.); 1922 transferred to W. J. Tatem Ltd.; 1934 to Barzilay and Benjamin, Turkey, renamed *Ulku*; 1935 to the Turkish Navy for use as a fleet collier and subsequently reduced to a bunkering hulk; 1960 deleted from Lloyd's Register.
Molton 1919-1938	3,091	1919 built by Ropner Shipbuilding and Repairing Co. (Stockton) Ltd., Stockton on Tees, as *Molton* for Lord Glanely; 1920 transferred to the Atlantic Shipping and Trading Co. Ltd. (W. J. Tatem Ltd.); 1922 transferred to W. J. Tatem Ltd.; 1938 to Continental Transit Co. Ltd., London, renamed *Transit*; 1939 to the Board of Trade (Sir William Reardon Smith and Sons Ltd.), London, renamed *Botusk*; 31.1.1941 mined and sunk off North Rona Island.
Monkton 1920-1929	3,088	1920 built by Ropner Shipbuilding and Repairing Co. (Stockton) Ltd., Stockton on Tees, as *Monkton* for Lord Glanely; 1920 transferred to the Atlantic Shipping and Trading Co. Ltd. (W. J. Tatem Ltd.); 1922 transferred to W. J. Tatem Ltd.; 1929 to Cia. Maritima Bilbao (E. Cortina), Spain, renamed *Indauchu*; 1935 management transferred to A. Opitz; 1938 transferred to Soc. Anon. Cooperativa di Nav. "Garibaldi", Italy, renamed *Sulmona* for the duration of the Spanish Civil War; 1939 returned to Cia. Maritima Bilbao (A. Opitz), Spain, renamed *Indauchu*; 1949 to Cia. Soc. Anonima Maritima Union, Spain; 1952 to Transland S.A., Spain; 14.10.1970 arrived at Piraeus for breaking up.
Pilton 1920-1938	3,063	1920 built by Tyne Iron Shipbuilding Co. Ltd., Newcastle upon Tyne; Laid down as *War Chine* for the Shipping Controller, but completed as *Pilton*

Name and Period in Fleet	Gross Tons	History
		for W. J. Tatem Ltd.; 1920 transferred to the Atlantic Shipping and Trading Co. Ltd. (W. J. Tatem Ltd.); 1922 transferred to W. J. Tatem Ltd.; 1938 to Rederi A/B Sigyn (H. Lundgren), Sweden, renamed *Siljan*; 26.9.1940 torpedoed and sunk about 250 miles West of Ireland by the German submarine *U46* whilst on a voyage from Cardiff to Lisbon with a cargo of coal.
Somerton 1920-1935	5,227	1920 built by Wm. Pickersgill and Sons Ltd., Sunderland; Laid down as *War Smilex* for the Shipping Controller, but completed as *Somerton* for the Atlantic Shipping and Trading Co. Ltd. (W. J. Tatem Ltd.); 1922 transferred to W. J. Tatem Ltd.; 1935 to the Heirs of the late L. Z. Cambanis, Greece, renamed *Mina L. Cambanis*; 1954 to Maritsa Navegacion Ltda., Costa Rica, renamed *Ais Nikolas*; 3.11.1958 arrived at Rotterdam from Yxpila with a cargo of timber and laid up after developing leaks and grounding during the voyage; 2.1959 broken up at Hendrik Ido Ambacht by Frank Rijsdijk Ind. Ond.
Paignton Notton 1920-1923	3,096	1920 built by Blyth Shipbuilding and Dry Dock Co. Ltd., Blyth Laid down as *War Minaret* for the Shipping Controller; purchased by Lord Glanely during construction and renamed *Paignton*; but completed as *Notton* for the Atlantic Shipping and Trading Co. Ltd. (W. J. Tatem Ltd.); 1922 transferred to W. J. Tatem Ltd.; 1923 to Soc. Algerienne de Nav. pour l'Afrique du Nord (Ch. Schiaffino et Cie.), France, renamed *Rose Schiaffino*; 1.1941 seized by the Royal Navy at Gibraltar and transferred to the Ministry of War Transport, managers—Mark Whitwill and Son Ltd.; 26.10.1941 sailed from Wabana bound for Cardiff with a cargo of iron ore and disappeared.
Buckleigh (2) 1925-1933	5,074	1925 built by Bartram and Sons Ltd., Sunderland, as *Buckleigh* for the Tatem Steam Navigation Co. Ltd. (W. J. Tatem Ltd.); 1933 to Scindia Steam

Name and Period in Fleet	Gross Tons	History
		Navigation Co. Ltd., Bombay, renamed *Jalamohan*; 1951 broken up at Bombay.
Chulmleigh (3) 1925-1933	5,076	1925 built by Bartram and Sons Ltd., Sunderland, as *Chulmleigh* for the Tatem Steam Navigation Co. Ltd. (W. J. Tatem Ltd.); 1933 to Scindia Steam Navigation Co. Ltd., Bombay, renamed *Jalarajan*; 14.1.1942 torpedoed and sunk by the Japanese submarine *I165* in position 00.12′S, 97.00′E whilst on a voyage from Singapore to Calcutta.
Ashleigh (2) 1925-1936	4,853	1925 built by Furness Shipbuilding Co. Ltd., Haverton Hill on Tees, as *Ashleigh* for the Tatem Steam Navigation Co. Ltd. (W. J. Tatem Ltd.); 1936 to Counties Ship Management Co. Ltd., London, renamed *Kingston Hill*; 1937 to Kassos Steam Navigation Co. Ltd. (Pnevmaticos, Rethymnis and Yannaghas), Greece, renamed *Stavros*; 1953 to Santiago Steamship Co. Ltd., Costa Rica, renamed *Atenas*; 1959 transferred to Panamanian flag; 1960 to Cia. de Nav. Victoria Neptuno S.A. (Teh Hu Steamship Co. Ltd.), Panama, renamed *Amu Darya*; 1962 broken up at Osaka.
Iddesleigh (2) 1927-1944	5,205	1927 built by R. Thompson and Sons Ltd., Sunderland, as *Iddesleigh* for the Tatem Steam Navigation Co. Ltd. (W. J. Tatem Ltd.); 17.8.1944 sunk by one-man torpedo ¾ mile South of 90 Buoy, off Langrune Assault area, Normandy.
Winkleigh (1) 1927-1939	5,055	1927 built by Wm. Pickersgill and Sons Ltd., Sunderland, as *Winkleigh* for the Tatem Steam Navigation Co. Ltd. (W. J. Tatem Ltd.); 8.9.1939 torpedoed and sunk in position 48.06′N, 18.12′W by the German submarine *U48* whilst on a voyage from Vancouver to Manchester with a cargo of grain and lumber.
Umberleigh 1927-1946	4,950	1927 built by William Gray and Co. Ltd., West Hartlepool, as *Umberleigh* for the Tatem Steam Navigation Co. Ltd. (W. J. Tatem Ltd.); 1946 to

Name and Period in Fleet	Gross Tons	History
		Bayswater Shipping Co. Ltd. (Lemos and Pateras Ltd.), London, renamed *Bayswater*; 1947 to Pandelis D. Pateras, Greece, renamed *Kyvernitis*; 1954 to Cia. Mar. Mariato S.A., Liberia, renamed *Nicolas II*; 1958 to Phoebus D. Kyprianou, Lebanon, renamed *Dimos*; 3.7.1960 arrived at Komura, Japan, for breaking up.
Monkleigh 1927-1947	5,203	1927 built by R. Thompson and Sons Ltd., Sunderland, as *Monkleigh* for the Tatem Steam Navigation Co. Ltd. (W. J. Tatem Ltd.); 1944 transferred to the Atlantic Shipping and Trading Co. Ltd. (W. J. Tatem Ltd.); 1947 to Dolphin Steamship Co. Ltd. (Stathatos and Co. Ltd.), London, renamed *Ionian Sea*; 1951 to Attica Shipping Co. S.A., Panama, renamed *Attica*; 1954 Faros Shipping Co. Ltd., London, appointed as managers; 1960 broken up at Hong Kong.
Goodleigh (1) 1928-1937	3,845	1928 built by R. Thompson and Sons Ltd., Sunderland, as *Goodleigh* for the Dulverton Steamship Co. Ltd. (W. J. Tatem Ltd.); 1937 to Rennert and Co. G.m.b.h. (Fisser and von Doornum), Germany, renamed *Christoph.v.Doornum*; 1939 owners restyled as Fisser and v. Doornum Reederei G.m.b.H. (Fisser and v. Doornum); 10.9.1939 seized at Botwood by the Royal Navy; 30.10.1939 placed under the Ministry of War Transport, managers—H. Chisholm, renamed *Empire Commerce*; 9.6.1940 mined and sunk 4 cables from Spit Buoy, near Margate.
Filleigh (1) 1928-1945	4,856	1928 built by Wm. Pickersgill and Sons Ltd., Sunderland, as *Filleigh* for the Atlantic Shipping and Trading Co. Ltd. (W. J. Tatem Ltd.); 18.4.1945 torpedoed and sunk 10 miles E.N.E. of North Foreland by the German submarine *U245* whilst on a voyage from London to Antwerp.
Everleigh 1930-1945	5,222	1930 built by Furness Shipbuilding Co. Ltd., Haverton Hill on Tees, as *Everleigh* for the Atlantic

Name and Period in Fleet	Gross Tons	History

| | | Shipping and Trading Co. Ltd. (W. J. Tatem Ltd.); 6.2.1945 torpedoed and sunk in position 50.30′N, 01.48′W by the German submarine *U101* whilst on a voyage from London to New York. |

Hadleigh
1930-1943 — 5,222 — 1930 built by Furness Shipbuilding Co. Ltd., Haverton Hill on Tees, as *Hadleigh* for the Atlantic Shipping and Trading Co. Ltd. (W. J. Tatem Ltd.); 16.3.1943 torpedoed and sunk in position 36.10′N, 00.30′W by the German submarine *U77*.

Northleigh
1937-1956 — 5,450 — 1937 built by Wm. Pickersgill and Sons Ltd., Sunderland, as *Northleigh* for W. J. Tatem Ltd.; 1940 transferred to the Atlantic Shipping and Trading Co. Ltd. (W. J. Tatem Ltd.); 1956 to Fir Steamship Co. Ltd. (Fir Line Ltd.), Hong Kong, renamed *China Fir*; 1957 transferred to Hong Kong Fir Shipping Co. Ltd. (Fir Line Ltd.), Hong Kong; 18.4.1961 wrecked at Tathong Point, six miles from Kowloon, whilst on a voyage from Mormugao to Kobe.

Chulmleigh
(4)
1938-1942 — 5,445 — 1938 built by Wm. Pickersgill and Sons Ltd., Sunderland, as *Chulmleigh* for the Dulverton Steamship Co. Ltd. (W. J. Tatem Ltd.); 1940 transferred to the Atlantic Shipping and Trading Co. Ltd. (W. J. Tatem Ltd.); 5.11.1942 wrecked off Spitzbergen whilst on a voyage from the United Kingdom to Archangel.

Lady Glanely
1938-1940 — 5,497 — 1938 built by Wm. Doxford and Sons Ltd., Sunderland, as *Lady Glanely* for the Tatem Steam Navigation Co. Ltd. (W. J. Tatem Ltd.); 2.12.1940 torpedoed and sunk 400 miles West of Ireland by the German submarine *U101* whilst on a voyage from Vancouver to London.

Goodleigh
(2)
1938-1940 — 5,448 — 1938 built by Wm. Pickersgill and Sons Ltd., Sunderland, as *Goodleigh* for the Tatem Steam Navigation Co. Ltd. (W. J. Tatem Ltd.); 2.12.1940

Name and Period in Fleet	Gross Tons	History
		torpedoed and sunk in position 55.02′N, 18.45′W by the German submarine *U52*.
Winkleigh (2) 1940-1960	5,468	1940 built by Wm. Pickersgill and Sons Ltd., Sunderland. as *Winkleigh* for W. J. Tatem Ltd.; 1960 to Saint Anthony Shipping Co. Ltd., Liberia, renamed *St. Anthony*; 1960 transferred to Lebanese flag; 20.2.1966 arrived at Valencia for breaking up.
Chulmleigh (5) 1946-1961	5,349	1946 built by Wm. Doxford and Sons Ltd., Sunderland; Launched as *Empire Northfleet* for the Ministry of War Transport, but completed as *Chulmleigh* for the Atlantic Shipping and Trading Co. Ltd. (W. J. Tatem Ltd.); 1961 to the Whalton Shipping Co. Ltd. (Stephens, Sutton Ltd.), Newcastle upon Tyne, renamed *Rugeley*; 1964 to Union Fair Shipping Co. Ltd., Hong Kong, and was to have been renamed *Madura*, however on 28.5.1964 the ship was driven ashore at Lanto after dragging her anchors during a typhoon at Hong Kong; 10.7.1964 refloated in a damaged condition, and broken up at Hong Kong.
Lord Glanely 1947-1960	5,640	1947 built by Wm. Pickersgill and Sons Ltd., Sunderland, as *Lord Glanely* for the Atlantic Shipping and Trading Co. Ltd. (W. J. Tatem Ltd.); 1960 to Gulf Steamships Ltd., Pakistan, renamed *Mehdi*; 1971 transferred to Gulf Shipping Corporation Ltd., Pakistan; 13.9.1973 beached at Gadani Beach for breaking up.
Filleigh (2) 1957-1963	5,668	1957 built by Bartram and Sons Ltd., Sunderland, as *Filleigh* for the Atlantic Shipping and Trading Co. Ltd. (W. J. Tatem Ltd.); 1963 to Corporacion Peruana de Vapore, Peru, renamed *Ucayali*; 1969 to Simaba Cia. Mar. S.A., Greece, renamed *Anna Maria S*; 20.5.1978 grounded 15 miles S.W. of Bornholm whilst on a voyage from Gdynia to Tripoli; 29.5.1978 refloated and arrived at Kiel the following day but was found to be damaged beyond repair; 10.1978 broken up at Hamburg by Eckhardt and Co. K.G.

Name and Period in Fleet	Gross Tons	History
Glanely 1960-1969	8,261	1960 built by Austin and Pickersgill Ltd., Sunderland, as *Glanely* for the Atlantic Shipping and Trading Co. Ltd. (W. J. Tatem Ltd.); 1969 to Douglas Steamship Co. Ltd. (D. Lapraik and Company), London, renamed *Inchona*; 1975 to Bardai Shipping Company, Greece, renamed *Alekos K*; 1978 to Alkistis Shipping Co. S.A., Greece, renamed *Aries*; 5.2.1982 arrived at Ithaka for laying up. 1987 reported that vessel is to be broken up.
Landwade 1961-1972	7,856	1961 built by Bartram and Sons Ltd., Sunderland, as *Landwade* for the Atlantic Shipping and Trading Co. Ltd. (W. J. Tatem Ltd.); 1972 to Tonia Maritime Co. Ltd. (Union Commercial Steamship Company), Cyprus, renamed *Marytonia*; 1976 to Karavos Cia. Naviera S.A., Greece, renamed *Swede Tonia*; 1981 to Ion Shipping Company, Greece, renamed *Uniluck*; 21.4.1984 sold by Public Auction on behalf of creditors to Dhirubhai Shah and Associate, Jamnagar for breaking up.
Exning 1965-1973	7,465	1965 built by Austin and Pickersgill Ltd., Sunderland, as *Exning* for the Atlantic Shipping and Trading Co. Ltd. (W. J. Tatem Ltd.); 1973 to Maravilia Compania Naviera S.A., Panama, renamed *Maritsa*; 1974 renamed *Maritsa III*; 1983 to Milky Way S.A., Panama, renamed *Cyprus Trader*; 6.4.1985 arrived at Gadani Beach for breaking up.

14. APPENDIX TWO
SHIPS OWNED BY THE MARITIME SHIPPING AND TRADING CO. LTD. (G. C. GIBSON).

Name and Period in Fleet	Gross Tons	History
Cutcombe 1919-1928	5,264	1918 built by Richardson, Duck and Co. Ltd., Stockton on Tees, as *War Ostrich* for the Shipping Controller, managers—Donaldson Bros. Ltd.; 1919 to the Maritime Shipping and Trading Co. Ltd. (G. C. Gibson), renamed *Cutcombe*; 1928 to The Ben Line Steamers Ltd. (W. Thomson and Company), Leith, renamed *Bennevis*; 9.12.1941 captured by Japanese naval forces off Hong Kong, taken to Hainan Island and renamed *Gyokuyo Maru*; 14.11.1944 torpedoed and sunk by U.S. submarine *Spadefish* in position 31.04′N, 123.56′E.
Appledore (2) 1929-1942	5,218	1929 built by Furness Shipbuilding Co. Ltd., Haverton Hill on Tees, as *Appledore* for the Maritime Shipping and Trading Co. Ltd. (G. C. Gibson); 1942 management transferred to Michalinos and Co. Ltd., London, upon their acquisition of the Company; 1951 to Cia. de Nav. Centrale S.A., Panama, renamed *Aeas*; 1956 to Transportes Maritimos Pacifico S.A., Panama, renamed *Tribeam*; 1960 broken up in Japan.

15. APPENDIX THREE
SHIPS MANAGED ON BEHALF OF THE MINISTRY OF WAR TRANSPORT

Name and Period in Fleet	Gross Tons	Name
Kirsten Maersk 1940-1942	2,252	1920 built by Odense Staalskibs, Odense, as *Kirsten Maersk* for Dampskibs-selskabet af 1912 (A. P. Moller), Denmark; 1934 lengthened and gross tonnage increased to 2,410; 6.6.1940 taken over by the Ministry of Shipping, later the Ministry of War Transport, managers—W. J. Tatem Ltd.; 1942 management transferred to Constants (South Wales) Ltd., London; 11.6.1945 returned to owners; 1947 to Rederibolaget Zachariassen and Company, Finland, renamed *Finnborg*; 12.6.1948 collided with the steamer *Southport* in position 49.55'N, 02.08'W and sank, whilst on a voyage from Sfax to Finland with a cargo of phosphate.
Empire Chaucer 1942	5,970	1942 built by Wm. Pickersgill and Sons Ltd., Sunderland, as *Empire Chaucer* for the Ministry of War Transport, managers—W. J. Tatem Ltd.; 17.10.1942 torpedoed and sunk by the German submarine *U504*, S.W. of Cape Agulhas, in position 40.20'S, 18.30'E.
Empire Service 1943-1945	7,060	1943 built by Lithgows Ltd., Port Glasgow, as *Empire Service* for the Ministry of War Transport, managers—W. J. Tatem Ltd.; 1945 management transferred to T. and J. Harrison, Liverpool; 1946 to Charente Steamship Co. Ltd. (T. and J. Harrison), Liverpool, renamed *Selector*; 1960 to Margalante Compania Naviera S.A., Lebanon, renamed *Margalante II*; 9.5.1961 arrived at Hirao, Japan, for breaking up.

Name and Period in Fleet	Gross Tons	Name
Empire Tudor 1944-1946	7,087	1944 built by Shipbuilding Corporation Ltd., Sunderland, as *Empire Tudor* for the Ministry of War Transport, managers—W. J. Tatem Ltd.; 1946 management transferred to Goulandris Bros. Ltd., London, renamed *Grandyke*; 1949 to the Ben Line Steamers Ltd. (Wm. Thomson and Company), Leith, renamed *Benvannoch*; 1956 to Helmville Ltd., London, renamed *Medina Princess*; 3.8.1962 ran aground on a reef near Djibouti, but later refloated and moored at Djibouti; 1.9.1964 broke adrift from her moorings and once again ran ashore, where she remained, part submerged; 1968 reported abandoned.